Abraham Clark Freeman

Void Execution, Judicial And Probate Sales, the Legal And Equitable Rights of Purchasers Thereat, etc.

And the constitutionality of special Legislation (Edition 2)

Abraham Clark Freeman

Void Execution, Judicial And Probate Sales, the Legal And Equitable Rights of Purchasers Thereat, etc.
And the constitutionality of special Legislation (Edition 2)

ISBN/EAN: 9783744731720

Printed in Europe, USA, Canada, Australia, Japan

Cover: Foto ©Suzi / pixelio.de

More available books at **www.hansebooks.com**

VOID

EXECUTION, JUDICIAL AND PROBATE

SALES,

—— AND THE LEGAL AND EQUITABLE ——

RIGHTS OF PURCHASERS THEREAT,

—— AND THE ——

CONSTITUTIONALITY OF SPECIAL LEGISLATION

VALIDATING VOID SALES, AND AUTHORIZING INVOLUN-
TARY SALES IN THE ABSENCE OF JUDICIAL
PROCEEDINGS.

SECOND EDITION.

By A. C. FREEMAN,

Author of Treatises on "Judgments," "Executions," "Cotenancy and Partition," Etc.

ST. LOUIS, MO.:
WILLIAM H. STEVENSON,
LAW PUBLISHER AND PUBLISHER OF THE
CENTRAL LAW JOURNAL.
1886.

TABLE OF CASES.

[The references are to sections.]

A.

Abbott v. Coburn,	4
Abbott v. Curran,	20
Ackley v. Dygert,	12, 17
Adams v. Jeffries,	15
Adams v. Morrison,	34
Adams v. Norris,	4
Adams v. Palmer,	61
Adams v. Smith,	49
Alabama Conference v. Price,	11
Ala. L. I. & T. Co. v. Boykin,	60
Aldrich v. Wilcox,	34
Alexander v. Miller's Ex.,	25
Alexander's Heirs v. Maverick,	8
Allen v. Kellam,	10
Allen v. Shepard,	20
Ameth v. Bailey,	11
Anderson v. Foulks,	48
Anderson v. Green,	33
Anderson v. Turner,	9
Andrews v. Avery,	4
Andrews v. Roberts,	1
Andrews v. Russell,	57
Andrews v. Scotton,	1
Angle v. Spear,	54
Armstrong v. McCoy,	47
Arnold v. Cord,	49
Arrowsmith v. Harmoning,	20
Ashurst v. Ashurst,	32
Atkins v. Kinnan,	11, 20, 47

B.

Babbitt v. Doe,	16
Babcock v. Cobb,	22
Bagley v. Ward,	24
Bailey v. Brown,	9
Bailey v. Robinson,	33
Bank v. Beatty,	29
Bank v. Dudley,	30
Bank v. Trapier,	31
Barbee v. Perkins,	20
Barelli v. Ganche	53
Barker, *ex parte*,	2, 10
Barnes v. Fenton,	41
Barnes v. Morris,	46
Barrett v. Churchill,	48
Barrett v. Gurney,	4
Barron v. Mayor of Baltimore,	62
Barron v. Mullin,	48
Bartee v. Tomkins,	48
Bartlett v. Judd,	55
Bartlett v. Sutherland,	9
Barton v. Hunter,	40
Bassett v. Lockwood,	48
Beach v. Walker,	60
Beal v. Harmon,	11
Beard v. Rowan,	9
Beauregard v. New Orleans,	15
Beckett v. Selover,	4, 5, 20
Beel v. Green,	27
Bell's Appeal,	9
Bennett, *ex parte*,	2
Benson v. Cilley,	8, 15
Bentley v. Long,	52
Bentz's Est.,	13
Bethel v. Bethel,	44
Bigelow v. Bigelow,	4
Bigelow v. Booth,	24
Bishop v. O'Conner,	51, 53
Bithson v. Budd,	47
Blackman v. Bauman,	22
Blair, *ex parte*,	9
Blair v. Campton,	30
Bland v. Bower,	53
Bland v. Muncaster,	9, 28, 33
Bledsoe v. Willingham,	26
Blodgett v. Hitt,	16, 28, 53
Blodgett v. Hubart,	53
Bloom v. Burdick,	11, 12, 20, 22
Blood v. Hayman,	41
Bobb v. Barnum,	47
Boggs v. Hargrave,	49
Boland's Estate,	11
Bolivar v. Zeiglar,	48
Bompart v. Lucas,	11
Boon v. Bowers,	68
Booth v. Booth,	60
Boren v. McGeehe,	23
Boring v. Lemmon,	45
Boro v. Harris,	48
Bouldin v. Ewart,	39
Bowen v. Bond,	13, 14
Bowen v. Jones,	29
Boyce v. Sinclair,	60
Boyd v. Blankman,	1, 20, 33
Boykin v. Cook,	48
Braddee v. Brownfield,	57
Branham v. San Jose,	49
Bray v. Marshall,	41

TABLE OF CASES CITED.

Bree v. Bree,	12, 18
Brenham v. Davidson,	66
Brenham v. Story,	72
Brevard v. Jones,	25
Brevoort v. Grace,	72
Bright v. Boyd,	53, 55
Brinton v. Seevers,	61
Brobst v. Brock,	52
Brock v. Frank,	4
Bronner v. Greenlee,	43
Brooks v. Rooney,	28, 47
Brown v. Brown,	20
Brown v. Armistead,	9
Brown v. Bond,	20
Brown v. Butters,	27
Brown v. Christie,	30
Brown v. Gilmor,	44
Brown v. Hobson,	9
Brown v. Lane,	49
Brown v. Redwyne,	8
Broughton v. Bradley,	4
Bryan v. Bauder,	11
Buchanan v. Tracy,	47
Bullard v. Hinkley,	36
Bull, Matter of,	68
Bunce v. Bunce,	18, 22
Burbank v. Simmes,	9
Burch v. Hantz,	33
Burdett v. Silsbee,	4
Burns v. Hamilton,	48, 49
Burns v. Leabetter,	48
Burton v. Lies,	49
Burton v. Spiers,	28, 60
Bybee v. Ashby,	29
Byers v. Fowler,	21
Byrd v. Turpin,	48

C.

Calder v. Bull,	56, 62
Caldwell v. Blake,	41
Campbell v. Brown,	16, 48
Campbell v. Knights,	22
Campbell v. P. S. I. Works,	38
Casey v. Gregory,	21
Cashion v. Farria,	48
Chandler v. Moulton,	33
Chase v. Ross,	10
Clark v. Sawyer,	47
Clark v. Thompson,	16, 17
Clark v. Van Surlay,	66, 68
Clingman v. Hophie,	24
Carpenter v. Pennsylvania,	62
Carpenter v. Sherfy,	46
Carroll v. Olmstead,	66
Carter v. Waugh,	20
Castleman v. Relfe,	43
Chambers v. Cochran,	49
Chambers v. Jones,	17, 29, 53
Chandler v. Northrop,	58
Chapman v. Brooklyn,	49
Chapman v. Harwood,	46
Chase v. Ross,	2, 10
Chesnut v. Shane,	62
Chesnut v. Shane's Lessee,	60
City of Portland v. City of Bangor,	62
Clark v. Thompson,	17
Clarke v. Van Surlay,	66, 68
Cochran v. Van Surlay,	68, 72
Cockey v. Cole,	41
Cofer v. Miller,	21
Coffin v. Cottle,	6
Cogan v. Foley,	48
Cogan v. Frisby,	48
Cobea v. State,	22
Colbert v. Moore,	48
Collars v. McLeod,	29
Collier's Admr. v. Windham,	24
Collins v. Montgomery,	31
Comstock v. Crawford,	15
Conklin v. Edgerton,	9
Conyers v. Meryeles,	54
Conover v. Musgrove,	44
Cook v. Travis,	38
Cook v. Toombs,	49
Cookerly v. Duncan,	60
Cooley v. Wilson,	21, 28
Coon v. Fry,	11, 12
Cooper v. Homer,	41
Cooper v. Reynolds,	5
Cooper v. Sunderland,	22
Copehart v. Downey,	48
Coppinger v. Rice,	4
Corbitt v. Clenny,	41
Core v. Strichler,	44
Cornwall's Estate,	11
Corwin v. Merritt,	11, 16, 19
Corwin v. Shoup,	50
Corbitt v. Clenny,	46
Coy v. Downie,	16
Crain v. Rothermel,	40
Crane v. Guthrie,	36
Cravens v. Moore,	2
Cromwell v. Hall,	20
Crosby v. Dowd,	20
Crouch v. Eveleth,	29
Crowell v. Meconkey,	50
Crusoe v. Butler,	9
Curley's Succession,	27, 28
Currie v. Stewart,	22
Curtis v. Norton,	43
Cutts v. Haskins,	4

D.

Dachmont v. Vaughan,	41
Dagger v. Taylor,	42
Dakin v. Demming,	3
Dakin v. Hudson,	16
Dale v. Medcalf,	59
Davenport v. Sovil,	51
Davenport v. Young,	69
Davidson v. Davidson,	33, 53
Davidson v. Koehler,	66
Davie v. McDaniel,	8
Davis v. Brandon,	46
Davis v. Gaines,	20, 53
Davis v. Helbig,	66
Davis v. Kline,	47
Davis v. Menasha,	57
Davis v. State Bank,	60
Davison v. Johonnot,	66, 69
Dawson v. Litsey,	34
Dean v. Morris,	48
De Bardelaben v. Stoudenmire,	10, 13
Deford v. Mercer,	50
De Forrest v. Farley,	21
De La Montagnie v. Union Ins. Co.,	9
Delaney's Estate,	9
Delaplaine v. Lawrence,	39
Dennis v. Winter,	44
Denny v. Mattoon,	57, 58
Dentzel v. Waldie,	60
De Riemer v. De Cantillon,	55
Dickerson v. Talbot,	43
Dickey v. Beatty,	55
Dodd v. Neilson,	48
Doe v. Anderson,	17
Doe v. Bowen,	8, 16
Doe v. Douglass,	67
Doe v. Hardy,	45
Doe v. Harvey,	8

TABLE OF CASES CITED.

Doe v. Henderson,	20
Doe v. Ingersoll,	23
Doe v. McLoskey,	15
Dohargue v. Cress,	50
Doolittle v. Holton,	8
Dorsey v. Gilbert,	66
Dougherty v. Linthicum,	36
Douglass v. Bennett	53
Douglass v. Haberstro,	25
Donner v. Smith,	4
Downing v. Rugar,	10
Draper v. Bryson,	28
Drefall v. Tuttle,	23
Dresbach v. Stein,	1, 43
Driggs v. Abbott,	4
Drinkwater v. Drinkwater,	38
Dubois v. McLean,	69
Du Chastellux v. Fairchild,	57
Dufour v. Camfranc,	47, 52
Dulany v. Tilghman,	60
Dunbar v. Creditors,	53
Duncan v. Stewart,	4
Dunn v. Frazier,	48, 49
Dunning v. O. N. B.,	9
Durham's Estate,	9
Duval's Heirs v. P. & M. Bank,	15
Dwight v. Blackmar,	33

E.

Eads v. Stephens,	31
Eberstein v. Oswalt,	36
Edmunds v. Crenshaw,	33
Edney v. Edney,	48
Edwards v. Pope,	71
Ellet v. Paxson,	32
Elliott v. Knott,	26
Ellsworth v. Hall,	11
Emory v. Vroman,	44
England v. Clark,	48
Estep v. Hutchinson,	66
Esthell v. Nichols,	11
Evans v. Chew,	9
Evans v. Snyder,	9, 53
Ewing v. Higby,	15, 44

F.

Fambro v. Gantt,	32
Farmers' Bank v. Martin,	48
Farmers' Bank v. Merchant,	45
Farnum v. Perry,	33
Furrar v. Dean,	11
Farrington v. King,	20
Fell v. Young,	8
Ferguson v. Williams,	62
Field's Heirs v. Goldsby,	15
Field v. Schieffelin,	9
Finch v. Edmonson,	11
Finley v. Grant,	23
Fisher v. Bassett,	4
Fiske v. Kellogg,	16
Fisk v. Norvel,	4, 7
Fitch v. Miller,	12, 13, 14
Fitch v. Witbeck,	10
Fitzpatrick v. Peabody,	21
Flanders v. Flanders,	33
Fleming v. Ball,	20
Fleming v. Powell,	45
Fletcher v. Peck,	62
Flinn v. Chase,	7
Florentine v. Barton	71
Foley v. Kane,	39
Forbes v. Halsey,	11
Ford v. Walsworth,	11, 12
Forman v. Hunt,	1

Forster v. Forster,	60
Foster v. Birch,	22
Foster v. Essex Bank,	62
Foster v. Mabe,	31
Frazier v. Steenrod,	18
Frederick v. Pacquetto,	10
French v. Currier,	9
French v. Edwards,	23
French v. Hoyt,	16
Froneberger v. Lewis,	33
Frost v. Yonkers,	5, 23
Fuller v. Little,	33
Fullerton v. McArthur,	71

G.

Gage v. Schroder,	21
Gager v. Henry,	15
Gaines v. De La Croix,	4, 32
Gaines v. Kennedy,	53
Gaines v. Fenton,	9
Galpin v. Page,	5
Gannett v. Leonard,	67, 70
Gardner v. Maroney,	20
Gay v. Minot,	6
Geddings v. Steele,	20
Gelstrop v. Moore,	9
George v. Watson,	15
Geruon v. Bestick,	28
Gerrard v. Johnson,	8
Gibbs v. Shaw,	8, 16
Gibson v. Roll,	7, 11, 18, 19
Gilbert v. Cooley,	52
Gilbert v. Hoffman,	54
Gilchrist v. Shackleford,	11
Giles v. Pratt,	41
Girard L. Ins. Co. v. F. & M. Bank	1
Glass v. Greathouse,	33
Glenn v. Wootten,	28
Glover v. Ruflin,	47
Gerrard v. Thompson,	16
Godbold v. Lambert,	24
Goforth v. Longworth,	9
Going v. Emery,	9
Good v. Norley,	16, 17
Goode v. Crow,	48
Goodbody v. Goodbody,	21
Goodman v. Winter,	53
Goodrich v. Pendleton,	4
Goodwin v. Jones,	9
Gordon v. Camp,	29
Gordon v. Gilfoil,	26
Gordon v. Gordon,	20
Gourdin v. Davis,	47
Gowan v. Jones,	43
Graham v. Hawkins,	20
Graham v. Lynn,	24
Grant v. Lloyd,	53, 54
Gray v. Hawes,	2
Grayson v. Weddle,	12, 20, 43, 55
Green v. Sargeant,	33
Greene v. Holt,	33
Gregory v. McPherson,	10, 11, 12
Gregory v. Taber,	11, 12, 13
Gridley v. Phillips,	46
Greer's Appeal,	10
Griffin v. Cunningham,	58
Griffith v. Fowler,	1
Griffith v. Frazier,	4, 7
Grignon's Lessee v. Astor,	14, 15
Grimes v. Doe,	57
Grimes v. Norris,	4
Griswold v. Bigelow,	47
Groff v. Jones,	34
Grogan v. San Francisco,	62
Gulley v. Prather,	9

TABLE OF CASES CITED.

Case	Page
Gurney's Succession,	20
Guerrero v. Ballerino,	33
Gunz v. Heffner,	2
Guy v. Pierson,	11
Gwin v. McCarroll,	8
Gwinn v. Williams,	41

H.

Case	Page
Halcombe v. Loudermilk,	49
Hall v. Chapman,	11
Hall v. Thayer,	6
Halleck v. Guy,	1, 44
Halleck v. Moss,	16, 18
Hamblin v. Warnecke,	33, 35
Hamilton v. Lockhart,	16, 22
Handy v. Noonan,	50
Hanks v. Neal,	5, 7, 28
Harlan's Estate,	4
Harlan v. Harlan,	25
Harriman's Heirs v. Janney,	41
Harrington v. O'Reilly,	24
Harris v. Corriell,	23
Hart v. Henderson,	58
Harris v. Lester,	21
Harrison v. Maxwell,	47
Harrison v. McHenry,	33
Haskins v. Wallit,	25, 47
Hastings v. Johnson,	34
Hatcher v. Briggs,	53
Hatcher v. Clifton,	20
Hathaway v. Heswell,	24
Havens v. Sherman,	17, 19
Haws v. Clark,	18
Hawkins v. Hawkins,	44
Hawkins v. Miller,	49
Haynes v. Meeks,	4, 11, 12, 13, 14, 53
Hays v. Jackson,	9
Hays v. McNealy,	11
Headen v. Oubre,	50
Hearth v. Wells,	20
Hedges v. Mace,	21
Helmer v. Rehm,	28
Helms v. Love,	19
Henderson v. Hays,	28
Henderson v. Herrod,	43
Henderson v. Overton,	49
Herbert v. Herbert,	47
Herdman v. Short,	18
Herndon v. Rice,	49
Herrick v. Ammerman,	20, 28
Herrman v. Fontelieu,	27
Heyman v. Babcock,	23
Hibberd v. Smith,	25, 41
Hicks v. Weens,	33
Hickson v. Rucker,	48
High v. Nelms,	38
Hightower v. Handlin,	34
Hill v. Billingsly,	53
Hill v. Town of Sunderland,	57
Hill v. Wall,	20
Hind's Heirs v. Scott,	47
Hite v. Taylor,	9
Hoard v. Hoard,	11
Hobart v. Upton,	28
Hobson v. Ewan,	43
Hoffman v. Strohtcher,	23
Holman's Heirs v. Bank of Norfolk,	67, 68, 69
Holman v. Gill,	41, 47
Holmes v. Shufer,	48
Holyoke v. Haskins,	4
Hopkins v. Mason,	58
Hoskins v. Helm,	24
Housley v. Lindsay,	48
Howard v. Moore,	46
Howard v. North,	28, 30, 49, 52
Howe v. McGivern,	35
Howell v. Tyler,	33
Hotchkiss v. Cutting,	44
Houx v. County of Bates,	55
Hoyt v. Sprague,	66
Hudgens v. Jackson,	28, 45
Hudgin v. Hudgin,	49, 53
Hughes v. Watt,	28
Humphrey v. Beeson,	47
Hurley v. Barnard,	8
Hurst v. Siford,	24
Hutchinson v. Cassidy,	32
Hutton v. Williams,	1

I.

Case	Page
Ikelheimer v. Chapman,	11
Irwin v. Scribner,	4
Islay v. Stewart,	48
Ives v. Ashley,	33

J.

Case	Page
Jackson v. Bowen,	52
Jackson v. Crawfords,	11, 12, 14
Jackson v. Robinson,	10, 11, 20
Jackson v. Summerville,	54
Jackson v. Todd,	9
Jackson v. Williams,	9
Jacob's Appeal,	44
Jaggers v. Griffin,	48
Jarboe v. Colvin,	21
Jarvis v. Russick,	29
Jayne v. Boisgerard,	53
Jefferson v. Curry,	30
Jelks v. Barrett,	55
Jennings v. Jennings,	48
Jennings v. Kee,	50
Jennings v. Moses,	4
Jochumsen v. Suffolk S. B.,	4
Johns v. Rome,	55
Johnson v. Bemis,	30
Johnson v Caldwell,	49
Johnson v. Cooper,	50
Johnson v. Johnson,	18
Johnson v. Fritz,	50
Johnson v. Jones,	11
Johnson v. Robertson,	49
Jones v. Clark,	41
Jones v. Edwards,	8
Jones v. Henry,	49
Jones v. Hollingsworth,	43
Jones v. K. B. Assn.,	39
Jones v. Levi,	17
Jones v. Manly,	53
Jones v. Perry,	65
Jones v. Warnoch,	48
Jones v. Taylor,	47
Jones v. Mortimer,	53
Journeay v. Gibson,	60
Julian v. Beal,	49

K.

Case	Page
Kable v. Mitchell,	43
Kane v. McCown,	30
Kane v. Paul,	4
Karnes v. Harper,	23
Kearney v. Taylor,	60
Kempe v. Pintard,	50
Kendall v. Miller,	9
Keepter v. Force,	54
Keith v. Keith,	47
Kennard v. Louisiana,	62

TABLE OF CASES CITED.

Case	Page
Kennedy v. Clayton,	31
Kennedy v. Gaines,	17
Kezar v. Elkins,	23
Kibby v. Chitwood,	67, 69
Kidwell v. Brummagim,	9
King v. Gunnison,	48
King v. Kent's Heirs,	13
Kingsbury v. Wild,	47
Kingston Bank v. Eltinge,	49
Kipp v. Bullard,	35
Kittredge v. Folsom,	4
Knott v. Stearns,	41
Koehler v. Ball,	44
Kostenbader v. Spotts,	48

L.

Case	Page
Lafferty v. Conn,	28
Lambertson v. Merchants' Bank,	39
Lamothe v. Lippott,	41
Lane v. Dorman,	69
Lane v. Nelson,	58, 60
Larco v. Casaneuava,	9
Larmeler v. McGinty,	50
Latimer v. R. R. Co.,	4
Laughman v. Thompson,	48
Laws v. Thompson,	49
Lee v. Gardner,	50
Leggett v. Hunter,	68, 72
Leland v. Wilson,	45
Lewis v. Dutton,	4
Lewis v. Owens,	54
Lewis v. Webb,	57
Levy v. Riley,	53
Lieby v. Ludlow,	51
Lincoln v. Alexander,	58
Lindsay v. Jaffray,	7
Litchfield v. Cudworth,	33, 34
Little v. Sinnet,	28
Livingston v. Cochran,	33
Loan Association v. Topeka,	56
Lockhart v. John,	22
Lockwood v. Stradley,	9
Lockwood v. Sturtevant,	34, 47
Lofland v. Ewing,	29
Logsdon v. Spevey,	30
London v. Robertson,	48
Long v. Burnett,	10
Long v. Wellar,	20, 48
Longworth v. Goforth,	50
Louisville v. University,	62
Low v. Purdy,	9
Ludlow v. Park,	35
Lynch v. Baxter,	1

M.

Case	Page
Macy v. Raymond,	30, 46
Maddox v. Sullivan,	28
Mahan v. Reeve,	55
Maina v. Elliott,	41
Maple v. Kussart,	50
Maple v. Nelson,	27
Mare v. Bradford,	28
Marr v. Boothby,	30
Marr v. Peay,	9
Martin v. Bonsach,	47
Martin v. Wilbourne,	47
Martin v. Tarver,	48
Mason v. Ham,	30, 46
Mason v. Osgood,	1, 43
Mather v. Chapman,	60
Matheson v. Hearin,	15
Matter of Bull,	68
Matter of Trustees of N. Y. P. E. Public School,	68
Maurr v. Parrish,	13, 18
Maxwell v. Goetschius,	58
Mayers v. Carter,	30
Mayor v. Horn,	61
Mays v. Wherry,	39
McAnnity v. McClay,	10
McArthur v. Carrie,	32
McBain v. McBain,	43
McBryde v. Wilkinson,	55
McCaskey v. Graff,	51
McCauley v. Harvey,	14
McCown v. Foster,	20
McDade v. Burch,	20
McDaniel v. Correll,	58
McFelly, Matter of,	28
McGavock v. Bell,	21
McGee v. Wallis,	53
McGhee v. Ellis,	49
McGill v. Doe,	38
McGuire v. Kouns,	47
McKeever v. Balt,	11, 12, 22
McKinney v. Jones,	22
McLaughlin v. Daniel,	52
McLaughlin v. Janney,	30
McLeod v. Johnson,	50
McManus v. Keith,	48
McNair v. Hunt,	28
McNeil v. First Cong. Church,	4, 10, 63
McPherson v. Cundiff,	15
McRae v. Dauner,	44
Mebane v. Layton,	35
Mebberly v. Johnson,	22
Mech. S. & B. Assn. v. O'Conner,	48
Melmas v. Pfisler,	22
Menges v. Dentler,	60, 61
Menges v. Wertman,	60, 61
Merrill v. Harris,	20
Merritt v. Horne,	50
Merrit v. Terry,	45
Michael v. McDermott,	32
Mickel v. Hicks,	15
Miles v. Wheeler,	33
Milford v. Beberidge,	21
Miller v. Babcock,	2
Miller v. Jones,	2, 10
Miller v. Kalb,	54
Miller v. Miller,	10
Millis v. Lombard,	21, 41
Minnesota Co. v. St. Paul Co.,	1, 44
Minor v. Selectmen,	28
Mitchell v. Bliss,	47
Mitchell v. Freedley,	50
Mitchell v. Ireland,	30
Mofitt v. Mofitt,	11, 13
Mohan v. Smith,	35
Mohr v. Manierre,	12, 15
Mohr v. Porter,	15
Mohr v. Tulip,	12, 50, 53
Monaghan v. Small,	48
Monahan v. Vandyke,	19
Monarque v. Monarque,	48
Monell v. Dennison,	4
Money v. Turnipseed,	20
Moody v. Butler,	21, 43
Montgomery v. Johnson,	15, 20
Moore v. Greene,	43
Moore v. Neil,	41
Moore v. Philbrick,	4
Moore v. Starks,	8, 17
Moore v. Wingate,	47
Moreau v. Branham,	55
Morgan v. Wattles,	33
Morrell v. Ingle,	31
Morris v. Hogle,	7, 11, 18
Morrow v. Weed,	13, 20, 28
Morton v. Welborn,	49

TABLE OF CASES CITED.

Moses v. McFarlane, 49
Mott v. Ackerman, 9
Mount v. Valle, 12
Mountour v. Purdy, 28
Muflitt v. Muflitt, 28
Muir v. Craig, 49
Mulford v. Beveridge, 17
Mulford v. Stalzenback, 20, 41
Muncie Bank v. Miller, 60
Munn v. Burges, 33
Munson v. Newson, 4
Murphy v. Hill, 31
Murphy v. Teter, 33
Murray v. Hoboken L. & I. Co., 62
Murrell v. Roberts, 23
Muskingum Bank v. Carpenter, 41
Musselman v. Eshelman, 33
Myer v. McDougal, 20, 41
Myers v. Davis, 20

N.

Neal v. Patterson, 32
Neligh v. Keene, 44
Nelson v. Carrington, 9
Nelson v. Rountree, 61, 62
Newcomb v. Smith, 11
Newman v. Samuel, 60, 61
Nicholl v. Nicholl, 22
Nowler v. Coet, 4, 51
Norris v. Clymer, 66
Norton v. Pettibone, 60
Nugent v. Gifford, 9

O.

Ogden v. Walters, 47
Opinion of the Judges, 65
Osgood v. Blackmore, 34
Osman v. Traphagen, 39, 44, 46
Osterberg v. U. F. Co., 48
Orton v. Noonan, 59
Overfield v. Bullett, 9
Overton v. Johnson, 12
Owens v. Hart, 35
Owen v. Slater, 48

P.

Paine v. Hoskins, 20
Parker v. Nichols, 22
Parmer v. Oakley, 22
Pattee v. Thomas, 12
Patterson v. Carneal, 34
Patterson v. Lemon, 21, 41
Paty v. Smith, 68
Payne v. Payne, 9
Pearce v. Patton, 60
Pearson v. Jamison, 29
Peebles v. Watts' Admr., 9
Pemberton v. McRae, 37
Penniman v. Cole, 24
Pennington v. Clifton, 49
People v. Platt, 62
Perkins v. Dibble, 47
Perkins v. Fairfield, 22
Perkins v. Gridley, 42
Perkins v. Winter, 15
Perry v. Clarkson, 30
Peters v. Caton, 30
Petrie v. Clark, 9
Phelps v. Buck, 10
Phillips v. Coffee, 47
Phillips v. Dana, 20
Piatt's Heirs v. McCullough's Heirs, 46
Pike v. Wassall, 44

Pinckney v. Smith, 15
Piper v. Elwood, 49
Potter v. Smith, 33
Powers v. Bergen, 72
Prater v. McDonough, 23
Pratt v. Houghtaling, 20
Price v. Boyd, 49
Price v. Johnson, 4
Price v. Winter, 17, 21
Pryor v. Downey, 10, 11, 58, 62
Puckett v. McDonald, 16
Pure v. Durall, 29
Pursley v. Hays, 50

R.

Ragland v. Green, 53
Randolph v. Bayue, 5
Raborg v. Hammond, 4
Rawlings v. Bailey, 43
Rea v. McEachron, 43
Rector v. Hartt, 39
Reed v. Austin, 23
Remick v. Butterfield, 33
Requa v. Holmes, 50
Reynolds v. Schmidt, 12
Reynolds v. Wilson, 28
Rheel v. Hicks, 49
Rice v. Parkman, 66
Richards v. Rote, 58
Richardson v. Vicker, 48
Richmond v. Marston, 49, 51
Ricketts v. Ungangst, 32
Riddle v. Hill, 48
Riddle v. Roll, 33
Riddle v. Turner, 24
Rigney v. Coles, 8
Rikeman v. Kohn, 24
Riley v. McCord, 4
Ritter v. Scammell, 41
Roberts v. Casey, 43
Robb v. Irwin, 15
Robbins v. Bates, 41
Robertson v. Bradford, 53
Robertson v. Johnson, 20, 43
Robinson v. Martel, 9
Roderigas v. East River S. I., 2, 4
Rogers v. Abbott, 53
Rogers v. Cawood, 30
Rogers v. Smith, 48
Rogers v. Wilson, 15
Rose's Estate, 11
Rose v. Newman, 29
Roseman v. Miller, 25
Root v. McFerrin, 8
Ross v. Luther, 25
Rozier v. Fagan, 69
Rucker v. Dyer, 22
Ruckle v. Barbour, 46
Rule v. Broach, 16
Rummels v. Kaylor, 54
Rumwell v. St. A. Bank, 11, 12
Russell v. Rumsey, 60
Ryden v. Jones, 33
Ryder v. Flanders, 11

S.

Sackett v. Twining, 1
Salmond v. Price, 49, 51
Sands v. Lynham, 53
Sandford v. Granger, 11
Sargent v. Sturm, 49
Satcher v. Satcher's Adm'r, 15
Satterlee v. Mathewson, 62
Schaefer v. Causey, 53

TABLE OF CASES CITED.

Savage v. Benham,	20	Steward v. Pettigrew,	28
Schneider v. McFarland,	16, 17	Steward v. Stocker,	24
Schnell v. Chicago,	18	Stewart v. Stokes,	55
Schindel v. Keedy,	1	Stillwell v. Swarthout,	18
Schwinger v. Hickok,	49	Stockton v. Downey,	53
Scott v. Bentel,	48	Stoltz's Succession,	27
Scott v. Dunn,	49, 53	Stow v. Kimball,	11, 20
Scott v. Freeland,	33	Strain v. Murphy,	47
Scott v. Gordon's Ex.,	33	Strong v. Beach,	54
Sebastian v. Johnson,	29	Stroble v. Smith,	50
Selsby v. Redlan,	60	Strouse v. Drennan,	11, 27
Seward v. Dideen,	8	Stuart v. Allen,	11, 12, 13, 14
Sexton v. Nevers,	49	Sumner v. Parker,	2, 10
Shaefer v. Gates,	2	Sutton v. Sutton,	4
Sharkey v. Bankston,	53	Suydam v. Williamson,	68
Shehan's Heirs v. Barnett's,	68, 69	Swan v. Wheeler,	29
Shelton v. Newton,	15	Swiggart v. Harber,	24
Sheldon v. Wright,	13, 47	Syndor v. Roberts,	21
Shelton v. Hamilton,	24	Sypert v. McCowen,	45
Sheppard v. Rhea,	30		
Sherman v. Buick,	72		
Sherwood v. Fleming,	61	**T.**	
Shoenberger v. School Directors,	72		
Short v. Porter,	48, 53	Tanner v. Stine,	47
Shouk v. Brown,	60	Taylor v. Connor,	49
Shriver v. Lynn,	44	Taylor v. Place,	57
Sibley v. Waffle,	16	Taylor v. Galloway,	9
Sigourney v. Sibley,	6	Taylor v. Taylor,	25
Silian v. Coffee,	23	Taylor v. Walker,	8, 16
Sinclair v. Jackson,	68	Tenney v. Poor,	11
Sittig v. Morgan,	50	Temple v. Cain	33
Sitzman v. Pacquette,	10	Terwilliger v. Brown,	33
Smith v. Arnold,	1	Tevis v. Pitcher,	4
Smith v. Calligan,	60	Thatcher v. Devoe	31
Smith v. Drake,	33	The Monte Allegro,	49
Smitha v. Flournoy,	11	Thomas v. Le Baron,	28, 47
Smith v. Finch,	47	Thomas v. Pullis,	66, 70
Smith v. Meldren,	39	Thompson v. Boardman,	9
Smith v. Mundy,	30	Thompson v. Davidson,	48
Smith v. Randall,	28	Thompson v. Morgan,	61
Smith v. Rice,	2	Thompson v. Munger,	48
Smith v. Schotts,	27	Thorn v. Ingram,	44
Smith v. Warden,	50	Thornton v. McGrath,	60, 62
Smith v. West,	43	Thornton v. Mulquinne,	22
Sneed v. Hooper,	9	Threlkelds v. Campbell,	48
Snevely v. Lowe,	15	Threff v. Fritz,	48
Snider v. Coleman,	53	Thurston v. Thurston,	66
Snowhill v. Snowhill,	66	Tiernan v. Beam,	55
Snyder v. Ives,	55	Tiernan v. Wilson,	34
Sohier v. M. G. Hospital,	57, 66, 71	Tilley v. Bridges,	48
Soloman v. Peters,	28	Tintal v. Drake,	67
Southard v. Perry,	50	Tippett v. Mize,	9, 30
Sharling v. Todd,	32	Tipton v. Powell,	43
Spaulding v. Baldwin,	8	Todd v. Dowd,	48
Specks v. Riggins,	47	Todd v. Flournoy,	67
Speck v. Wohlien,	42	Tongue v. Morton,	15
Spellman v. Dow,	10	Tooley v. Gridley,	50
Spragg v. Shriver,	50	Towle v. Forney,	68
Spragins v. Taylor,	20	Townsend v. Gordon,	12
Sprigg's Estate,	20	Townsend v. Tallant,	17, 18, 19, 44, 50
Spring v. Kane,	15, 21	Trent v. Trent,	11
Stampley v. King,	5, 17	Tremble v. Williams,	11
Stanley v. Noble,	4	Truse v. Old,	9
Staples v. Staples,	41	Tucker v. Harris,	8
Stapp v. Toler,	33	Turney v. Turney,	7, 11
State v. Doherty,	58	Tuttle v. Heavy,	9
State v. Newark,	62	Teverbangh v. Hawkins,	11
State v. Squires,	58, 62	Tyrrell v. Morris,	32
State v. Stanley,	50		
State v. Towl,	43	**U.**	
State v. Founts,	29		
State Bank v. Abbott,	54		
Steele's Ex. v. Moxley,	9	Underwood v. Lilly,	57
Stevens v. Enders,	58	Underwood v. McVeigh,	40
Stevens v. Hauser,	38	United States v. Arredondo,	2
Stevenson's Heirs v. McKeary,	8	United States v. Cruikshank,	62
Stewart v. Griffith,	66	Unknown Heirs v. Baker,	2

V.

Case	Page
Vallo v. Fleming,	8, 16, 43, 50, 53
Van Alstyne v. Wimple,	45
Van Campen v. Snyder,	23
Vandever v. Baker,	1
Varney v. Bevil,	4
Verdin v. Slocum,	48
Verry v. McClellan,	11
Vick v. Mayor,	16

W.

Case	Page
Wade v. Carpenter,	43
Wakefield v. Campbell,	34
Walpole v. Elliott,	57
Walker v. McKnight,	21
Walker v. Morris,	20
Walker v. Mulvean,	50
Wallace v. Loomis,	21, 41
Wallace v. Nichols,	41
Walsh v. Anderson,	41
Ward v. Bremer,	55
Ward v. Oats,	4
Ware v. Johnson,	55
Wales v. Willard,	7
Walker v. Sauvinet,	62
Wallace v. Hall,	43
Warfield's Estate,	4
Warner v. Helm,	49
Washburn v. Carmichael,	16
Washington v. McCaughan,	10, 22, 48
Watkins v. Holman,	67, 68, 69
Watson v. Mercer,	60, 62
Watson v. Oates,	67
Watson v. Reissig,	49
Wattles v. Hyde,	11
Watts v. Cook,	22
Watts v. Scott,	43
Watts v. Waddle,	4
Weaver v. Guyer,	34
Weed v. Donovan,	60
Weed v. Edmonds,	11
Wehrle v. Wehrle,	35
Weister v. Hade,	62
Welch v. Battern,	24
Welch v. Lewis,	21
Wellman v. Lawrence,	30, 46
Wells v. Chaflin,	9
Wells v. Polk,	20
West v. Waddell,	33
Weston v. Clark,	23
White v. Iseton,	33
White Mt. R. R. v. White Mts. R. R.	59
Whitman v. Fisher,	8, 41
Whitman v. Taylor,	21
Wier v. Davis,	32
Wight v. Wallbaum,	4
Wildes v. Vanvoorhis,	60
Wiley v. White,	22
Wilkerson v. Allen,	44
Wilkinson v. Filby,	22, 50
Wilkinson v. Leland,	56
Williams v. Childress,	11
Williams v. Morton,	21
Williams v. Reed,	22
Williams v. Warren,	11
Williams v. Williard,	50
Williams v. Woodman,	47
Williamson v. Ball,	68
Williamson v. Berry,	21, 42, 68
Williamson v. I. P. Congregation,	68
Williamson v. Branch Bank,	9
Williamson v. Williamson,	21, 30, 53, 67, 69
Willard v. Nason,	38
Willis v. Nicholson,	44
Willis v. Cowper,	4
Wilson v. Bigger,	50
Wilson v. Campbell,	25
Wilson v. Hastings,	11, 13
Wilson v. Twitty,	39
Winchester v. Winchester,	21
Wing v. Dodge,	13
Winslow v. Crowell,	53
Winston v. McFendon,	16, 17
Wisdom v. Parker,	41
Wisner v. Brown,	16
Withers v. Patterson,	2, 4, 10, 11, 62
Woltord v. Dugan,	25
Wood v. Augustine,	26
Wood v. Colvin,	23
Wood v. Crawford,	8
Wood v. McChesney,	11
Woodbury v. Parker,	33
Woodruff v. Cook,	11
Woods v. Monroe,	12, 19
Wooters v. Arledge,	37
Worten v. Howard,	32
Worthington v. Duncan,	11
Worthington v. McRoberts,	48
Wortman v. Skinner,	55
Wright v. Edwards,	11
Wright v. Hawkins,	61
Wright v. Ware,	11, 13, 20
Wyatts' Adm'r v. Rambo,	11, 20
Wyant v. Tuthill,	30, 44
Wyman v. Campbell,	22
Wynns v. Alexander,	32

Y.

Case	Page
Yarboro v. Brewster,	35
Yeomans v. Brown,	19, 20
Young v. Dowling,	55
Youngblood v. Cunningham,	25
Young v. Young,	11

Z.

Case	Page
Zebach v. Smith,	9
Zeigler v. Shorns,	41
Zuver v. Clark,	27

CHAPTER I.

INTRODUCTORY.

§ 1. Plan and Scope of the Work—Sundry Definitions. —We propose, in the following pages, to direct our attention, and that of our readers, to void execution and judicial sales, and the legal and equitable rights of purchasers thereat. Having considered these questions, we shall conclude with inquiries concerning the constitutionality of those curative acts, and that class of special legislation, which attempt either to validate invalid judicial sales, or to authorize involuntary sales, in the absence of any judicial proceedings whatever. In the terms "judicial and execution sales," as we here use them, are embraced all sales made in pursuance of the orders, judgments or decrees of courts, or to obtain satisfaction of such orders, judgments or decrees. Precisely what sales can accurately be denominated "judicial," is not very well settled. Of course they must be the result of judicial proceedings, and the order, decree or judgment on which they are based, must direct the sale of the property sold. There can be no judicial sale except on a pre-existing order of sale.[1] And probably the order of sale is not, alone, sufficient to entitle the sale to be called judicial. In a State where an administrator's sale, though

---

[1] Minnesota Co. v. St. Paul Co., 2 Wall. 640.

made by virtue of an order of court, was not required to be reported to the court nor to be confirmed, Judge Story held it not to be a judicial sale.[1] If, however, a sale is ordered by the court, is conducted by an officer appointed by, or subject to the control of the court, and requires the approval of the court before it can be treated as final, then it is clearly a judicial sale. Such a sale is unquestionably a sale by the court.[2] Sales made in proceedings for partition are undoubtedly judicial;[3] so are sales made by administrators and guardians under the practice pursued in most of the States.[4] Execution sales are not judicial.[5] They must, it is true, be supported by a judgment, decree or order. But the judgment is not for the sale of any specific property. It is only for the recovery of a designated sum of money. The court gives no directions, and can give none concerning what property shall be levied upon. It usually has no control over the sale beyond setting it aside for non-compliance with the directions of the statutes of the State. The chief difference between execution and judicial sales, are these: the former are based on a general judgment for so much money, the latter on an order to sell specific property; the former are conducted by an officer of the law in pursuance of the directions of a statute, the latter are made by the agent of a court in pursuance of the directions of the court; in the former the sheriff is the vendor, in the latter, the court; in the former the sale is usually complete when the property is struck off to the highest bidder, in the latter it must be reported to

---

[1] Smith v. Arnold, 5 Mason, 420.

[2] Forman v. Hunt, 3 Dana, 621.

[3] Freeman on Cotenancy and Partition, sec. 548; Hutton v. Williams, 35 Ala. 503; Girard L. Ins. Co. v. F. & M. Bank, 57 Pa. St. 388.

[4] Vandever v. Baker, 13 Pa. St. 121; Sackett v. Twining, 18 Pa. St. 199; s. c., 57 Am. Dec. 599; Halleck v. Guy, 9 Cal. 195; s. c., 70 Am. Dec. 643; Hutton v. Williams, 35 Ala. 517; Moore v. Shultz, 13 Pa. St. 98; s. c., 53 Am. Dec. 446; Lynch v. Baxter, 4 Tex. 431; s. c., 51 Am. Dec. 735; Mason v. Osgood, 64 N. C. 467.

[5] Griffith v. Fowler, 18 Vt. 394.

and approved by the court.[1] But our present purpose does not require us to announce any tests by which to determine what sales are judicial, nor to separate the different classes of judicial sales from one another. We shall assume that judicial sales embrace: 1st, those made in chancery; 2d, those made by executors, administrators and guardians, when acting by virtue of authority derived from orders of sale obtained in judicial proceedings; and, 3d, all other cases where property is sold under an order or decree of court designating such property and authorizing its sale. Void sales, whether execution or judicial, may, for convenience of treatment, be divided into two great classes: 1st, those which are void because the court had no authority to enter the judgment or order of sale; 2d, those which, though based on a valid judgment or order of sale, are invalid from some vice in the subsequent proceedings. The word void, though apparently free from ambiguity, is employed in various senses. Accurately speaking, a thing is not void unless it has no force or effect whatever. "A conveyance can not be said to be utterly void, unless it is of no effect whatsoever, and is incapable of confirmation or ratification."[2] "Another test of a void act or deed is, that every stranger may take advantage of it, but not of a voidable one. Again, a thing may be void in several degrees: 1st, void, so as if never done, to all purposes, so that all persons may take advantage thereof; 2d, void to some purposes only; 3d, so void by operation of law that he that will have the benefit of it may make it good."[3] In the terms "void sales," as employed in this work, we include all those sales which, as

---

[1] Andrews v. Scotton, 2 Bland, 636; Schindel v. Keedy, 43 Md. 417. A sale made by assignees acting under an assignment for the benefit of creditors, is, in Ohio, a judicial sale, because the proceedings and sale are, by the statute of that State, required to be conducted under the supervision and subject to the confirmation of the probate court. Dresback v. Stein, 41 Ohio St. 70.

[2] Boyd v. Blankman, 29 Cal. 35.

[3] Anderson v. Roberts, 18 Johns. 527; s. c., 9 Am. Dec. 235.

against the original purchaser, may, without any proceedings to set them aside, be treated as not transferring the title of the property assumed to be sold. These sales, it will be shown, may be ratified or confirmed. Many of them give rise to important equitable rights in favor of the original purchaser or his grantees. Some of them, while conferring neither legal nor equitable rights on the original purchaser, become, in the hands of his innocent vendees for value, in good faith and without notice, valid both at law and in equity.

CHAPTER II.

SALES VOID BECAUSE THE COURT HAD NO AUTHORITY TO ENTER THE JUDGMENT, OR ORDER OF SALE.

SECTION.
2. Jurisdiction, and the Effect of a Want of.
3. Kinds and Sources of Jurisdiction.
4. Instances of Want of Jurisdiction of Probate Courts over the Subject-matter.
5. Means of Acquiring Jurisdiction.
6. Cases in which the Judge is Disqualified from Acting.
7. Suspension or Loss of Jurisdiction.
8. General Principles Governing Questions of Jurisdiction.

ORDERS OF SALE IN PROBATE, AND HOW AUTHORITY TO MAKE MUST BE OBTAINED.

9. When Sales may be made without any License of Court.
10. Petition for License must be by Person Competent to Present it.
11. Sufficient Petition is Indispensable; what Petitions are Sufficient.
12. Statutes Designating what Petition must Contain.
13. Petitions for Sales Liberally Construed;—Referring to other Papers.
14. Not Fatal that Petition is not, in fact, True.
15. Notice of Application to Sell, Cases Holding it Unnecessary.
16. Notice of Application to Sell, Cases Holding it Necessary.
17. Notice of Application; Service on Minor not to be Waived nor Dispensed with.
18. Notice of Application must be given in the Manner Prescribed by Law.
19. Notice of Application must be given for the Time Prescribed by Law.
20. The License, or Order to Sell, and its Effect as an Adjudication.

§ 2. **The Effect of Want of Jurisdiction.**—A void judgment, order or decree, in whatever tribunal it may be entered, is, in legal effect, nothing. "All acts performed under it, and all claims flowing out of it, are void."[1] Hence, a sale, based on such a judgment, has no foundation in law. It must certainly fall.[2] Judicial proceedings are void when the court, wherein they take place, is acting without jurisdiction. "The power to hear and determine a cause is jurisdiction; it is *coram judice* whenever a cause is presented which brings this power into action; if the petitioner states such a case in his petition, that on a demurrer the court would render judgment in his favor, it is an undoubted case of jurisdiction."[3] "It is, in truth, the power to do both or either—to hear without determining, or to determine without hearing."[4] It must be constantly remembered that jurisdiction is indispensable to the validity of all judicial proceedings; that if the proceedings taken to obtain jurisdiction are radically defective, all subsequent steps are unavailing, however regular they may be. Thus, though the proceedings in a probate court to obtain an order of sale, and also the proceedings subsequent to the order, be all perfectly regular, yet the sale is utterly void, if it can be shown that there was no valid grant of administration, because the court had no jurisdiction to grant it.[5]

---

[1] Freeman on Judgments, sec. 117.

[2] Freeman on Executions, sec. 16, note 2; Gray v. Hawes, 8 Cal. 562; Gunz v. Heffner, 22 N. W. Rep. 386; Shaefer v. Gates, 2 B. Mon. 453; s. c., 38 Am. Dec. 164; Cravens v. Moore, 61 Mo. 178. A sale under a void judgment does not entitle the purchaser to the benefit of a statute requiring actions to be brought "within five years, where the defendant claims title to the land in question, by or through some deed made upon a sale thereof by an executor, administrator or guardian, or by a sheriff or other proper ministerial officer under the order, judgment, decree or process of a court or legal tribunal of competent jurisdiction within this State." Millar v. Babcock, 29 Mich. 526.

[3] United States v. Arredondo, 6 Pet. 709.

[4] *Ex parte* Bennett, 44 Cal. 88.

[5] Sumner v. Parker, 7 Mass. 79; Unknown Heirs v. Baker, 23 Ill. 490; Smith v. Rice, 11 Mass. 507; Chase v. Ross, 36 Wis. 267; Withers v. Patterson, 27 Tex. 501; *Ex parte* Baker, 2 Leigh, 719; Miller v. Jones, 26 Ala. 247. (See sec. 10.)

It may also be shown that an apparent grant of administration was not the act of the court or judge, but of the clerk or of some other person, who used blanks signed by the judge. Judicial authority cannot be delegated; and, although the judge left signed blanks with the clerk, intending for the latter to fill them up, and issue or enter them as the act of the court, still the clerk's act is not judicial, and his grant of administration is not binding as a judicial act.[1]

§ 3. **Kinds and Sources of Jurisdiction.**—"Jurisdiction is conferred upon courts by the constitution and laws of the country in which they are situate, authorizing them to hear and determine causes between parties, and to carry their judgments into effect."[2] The power to hear a particular class of cases, or to determine controversies of a specified character, is called jurisdiction over the subject-matter. This jurisdiction is conferred by the "authority which organizes the court, and is to be sought for in the general nature of its powers, or in authority specially conferred by statute. If the order or judgment, on which a sale was made, was one resulting from a controversy which the court had, in no circumstances, any power to determine, there was an absence of jurisdiction over the subject-matter, and the sale is incurably void."[3] In addition to jurisdiction over the subject-matter, it is also indispensable that the court should have jurisdiction over the person or thing against which its judgment operates. Jurisdiction over a subject-matter must be conferred by law;[4] jurisdiction over a person may be conferred by his consent. If jurisdiction over a person is not conferred by his consent, or obtained in the manner designated by law, the judgment against him is void, and can support no sale of his property.

[1] Roderigas v. East River Sav. Inst., 76 N. Y. 316; s. c., 32 Am. Rep. 309.
[2] Freeman on Judgments, sec. 119.
[3] Ibid., sec. 120.
[4] Dakin v. Demming, 6 Pai. 95.

§ 4. **Instances of Want of Jurisdiction over the Subject-matter** are found more frequently in *probate proceedings* than elsewhere. If the statute of a State, governing the settlement and distribution of the estates of deceased persons, makes no provision concerning the estates of persons who died prior to the passage of such statute, then an attempt to administer on one of the last named estates would be usurping authority over a subject-matter not within the jurisdiction of the court, and the proceedings would therefore be invalid.[1] So, if a probate court should make an order for the sale of property situate in another State than the one in which the order is made, this would also be an assumption of authority over a subject-matter not within the jurisdiction of the court, and would be void.[2] This rule has been held to be applicable even where personal property, though in another State at the death of its owner, was subsequently brought within the State where the order was made.[3] Courts of probate have no power to grant letters of administration, nor letters testamentary, on the estate of a living person. Letters may be granted, under a mistake of fact, upon the supposition that the testator, or other person, is dead. The case is nevertheless one in which the court has no jurisdiction. If he who was supposed to have died is, in fact, living, all probate sales and other proceedings are void, and can have no effect on his title.[4] Grants of letters of administration were for-

---

[1] Downer v. Smith, 24 Cal. 114; Coppinger v. Rice, 33 Cal. 408; Grimes v. Norris, 6 Cal. 621; s. c., 65 Am. Dec. 545; Adams v. Norris, 23 How. U. S. 353; Tevis v. Pitcher, 10 Cal. 465; McNeil v. First, 4 W. C. Rep. 421.

[2] Nowler v. Coit, 1 Oh. 519; s. c., 13 Am. Dec. 640; Salmond v. Price, 13 Oh. 368; s. c., 42 Am. Dec. 204; Watts v. Waddle, 6 Pet. 389; Wills v. Cowper, 2 Oh. 124; Latimer v. R. R. Co., 43 Mo. 105; Price v. Johnson, 1 Oh. St. 390.

[3] Varner v. Bevil, 17 Ala. 286,

[4] Duncan v. Stewart, 25 Ala. 408; s. c., 60 Am. Dec. 527; Griffith v. Frazier, 8 Cranch, 9; Fiske v. Norvel, 9 Tex. 13; s. c., 58 Am. Dec. 128; Jochumsen v. Suffolk Sav. Bank, 3 Allen, 87; Withers v. Patterson, 27

merly judged to be void unless the deceased did, in fact, die intestate.¹ Surrogate and probate courts are usually limited in their jurisdiction to a specified class of cases. Thus, it is generally required that a man's estate be settled in the county where he resided at the time of his death. If it appears that letters testamentary or of administration were granted in a county in which the deceased did not reside, the whole proceedings must be regarded as void.² How, and in what circumstances this fact may be made to appear, are questions to which diverse answers may be found in the authorities. Undoubtedly the records of the court may be inspected. If they show the non-residence of the deceased, they are competent evidence of their own invalidity. If

---

Tex. 496; Beckett v. Selover, 7 Cal. 215; s. c., 68 Am. Dec., 237; but a majority of the court of appeals of New York declared, in Roderigas v. East River Sav. Inst., 63 N. Y. 460; s. c., 20 Am. Rep. 555, that a grant of administration upon the estate of a living person was not void; but see a further decision in the same case, 76 N. Y. 316; s. c., 32 Am. Rep. 309.

¹ Holyoke v. Haskins, 5 Pick. 24; s. c., 16 Am. Dec. 372; Brock v. Frank, 51 Ala. 91; Kane v. Paul, 14 Pet. 39; Griffith v. Frazier, 8 Cranch, 24. This rule is believed to be obsolete in the United States. In its stead we have adopted the rule that a grant of administration, made by a court having jurisdiction of the subject-matter and of the particular case, while it remains unrevoked, cannot be regarded as void. "Nor can the recall or repeal of the appointment be fairly regarded as placing the appointees of the court in the same position as if the decree never existed. On the contrary, all acts done in the due course of administration, while such decrees remained in force, must be held entirely valid." Redfield on Wills, Part II, p. 109; Bigelow v. Bigelow, 4 Oh. 138; s. c., 19 Am. Dec. 597; Kittredge v. Folsom. 8 N. H. 98; Ward v. Oakes, 42 Ala. 225; Jennings v. Moses, 38 Ala. 402; Broughton v. Bradley, 34 Ala. 694; Brock v. Frank, 51 Ala. 91. But one who deals with an executor is not protected if he has notice of the existence of a later will than the one admitted to probate. Gaines v. De La Croix, 6 Wall. 720.

² Beckett v. Selover, 7 Cal. 215; s. c., 68 Am. Dec. 237; Haynes v. Meeks, 10 Cal. 110; s. c., 70 Am. Dec. 703; Harlan's Estate, 24 Cal. 182; Moore v. Philbrick, 32 Me. 102; s. c., 52 Am. Dec. 642; Munson v. Newson, 9 Tex. 109; Cutts v. Haskins, 9 Mass. 543; Holyoke v. Haskins, 5 Pick. 20, and 9 Pick. 259; s. c., 16 Am. Dec. 372; Goodrich v. Pendleton, 4 Johns. Ch. 549.

they fail to assert anything about the residence, either in the averments of the petition or in the findings of the court, we should judge this to be fatal. In every case it ought to appear, *prima facie*, that the court has jurisdiction over the estate. Usually a petition is presented to the court or judge, in which the facts authorizing the assumption of jurisdiction in the particular case are stated. The duty of the court or judge is to investigate and determine the truth of these jurisdictional allegations. Its subsequent grant of letters implies that these allegations have been found to be true. "Whenever the jurisdiction of a court not of record depends on a fact which it is required to ascertain and settle by its decision, such decision, if the court has jurisdiction of the parties, is conclusive, and not subject to any collateral attack."[1] Hence, in a case where a probate court has, upon a petition asserting the essential jurisdictional facts, and after notice to the parties in interest, given, in the manner prescribed by law, granted letters testamentary or of administration, the proceedings can not be avoided collaterally, in the majority of the States, by proof that the deceased did not die within the jurisdiction of the court.[2] Any other rule would lead to the most embarrassing results. The residence of a deceased person can be determined only by hearing parol evidence. Different judges may reach opposite conclusions from the same evidence. The parties in interest may at separate times produce different evidence on the same issue. If, after a court had heard and decided the issue concerning the residence of the deceased, the

---

[1] Freeman on Judgments, sec. 523.
[2] Irwin v. Scribner, 18 Cal. 499; Lewis v. Dutton, 8 How. Pr. 103; Andrews v. Avery, 14 Gratt. 236; Warfield's Estate, 2 Cal. 51; Sutton v. Sutton, 13 Vt. 71; Fisher v. Bassett, 9 Leigh, 119; s. c., 33 Am. Dec. 227; Barrett v. Garney, 33 Cal. 530; Driggs v. Abbott, 27 Vt. 581; Burdett v. Silsbee, 15 Tex. 615; Monell v. Dennison, 17 How. Pr. 422; Abbott v. Coburn, 28 Vt. 663; s. c., 67 Am. Dec. 735; Rarborg v. Hammond, 2 H. & G. 42. See also Riley v. McCord, 21 Mo. 265; Wight v. Wallbaum, 39 Ill. 554.

question remained unsettled to such an extent that it could be re-litigated for the purpose of avoiding all the proceedings of the court, no person would have the temerity to deal with executors or administrators.

§ 5. **Methods of Acquiring Jurisdiction.**—Jurisdiction over a complainant is obtained by his coming before the court and making his complaint in a manner recognized by law. This is usually by a statement in writing, filed in the court or with the clerk thereof. Jurisdiction over the defendant is obtained by his voluntary appearance in the action, or by the service of process upon him. Jurisdiction over a thing proceeded against *in rem* is acquired by its seizure under the process of the court.[1] If a defendant neither appears, nor is served with process, a judgment against him is void. If, however, he is served with process which is irregular in form, or the mode of service is irregular, he must generally object to such irregularity; if he fails to do so, and judgment is entered against him, it will generally not be treated as void, when collaterally assailed.[2] When letters testamentary or of administration on the estate of a deceased person, or of guardianship upon the person or estate of a lunatic or minor, are applied for, such measures as the statutes require must be taken for the purpose of obtaining jurisdiction over the persons interested. The statute may authorize the court to proceed without notice to any one. The proceeding may be *in rem*. But if notice is exacted by the statute, either by publication, or by the personal service of a citation, a substantial compliance with the statute is a pre-requisite to obtaining authority to proceed.[3]

---

[1] Cooper v. Reynolds, 10 Wall. 308; Galpin v. Page, 1 Cent. L. J. 491; 1 Saw. 309; 18 Wall. 350; Freeman on Judgments, secs. 606 and 611.

[2] Freeman on Judgments, sec. 126; Hanks v. Neal, 44 Miss. 224; Stampley v. King, 51 Miss. 738.

[3] Randolph v. Bayne, 44 Cal. 370; Beckett v. Selover, 7 Cal. 215; s. c., 68 Am. Dec. 267.

§ 6. **Where the Judge is Disqualified from Acting.**—Sometimes a court has jurisdiction, both over the person and the subject-matter, but cannot proceed because the judge thereof is disqualified from acting in the particular case. If, however, he proceeds, when incompetent by statute, his judgment or order is, in most States, invalid. For the purpose of trying or determining the particular matter, he is not a judge.[1]

§ 7. **Suspension or Loss of Jurisdiction.**—A court or judge having authority to proceed at one time may be divested of its jurisdiction, either temporarily or permanently. The court may be abolished, or its jurisdiction may be divested by statute. The proceedings may be removed into some appellate tribunal. The term of the court may be adjourned *sine die;* in which case no judgment can be entered before the re-opening of the court at its next term, unless expressly authorized by statute. In all cases where a court is rendered incompetent to proceed, its proceedings during such incompetency are as invalid as though it had never possessed jurisdiction.[2] If a probate court appoints an executor or administrator, it cannot, while he continues in office, appoint another. Its jurisdiction is exhausted. Its further grant of letters is void.[3] Neither can it appoint another administrator after an estate has been fully administered upon, and distributed to the heirs.[4] Where a statute forbade the administration upon the estates of persons who had been dead for more than twenty years, a grant of administration in defiance of the statute was adjudged void.[5] If notice is given that a petition for the sale of lands will be presented at a time specified, and it is not

---

[1] Freeman on Judgments, sec. 145; Sigourney v. Sibley, 21 Pick. 101; s. c., 32 Am. Dec. 248; Coffin v. Cottle, 9 Pick. 287; Hall v. Thayer, 105 Mass. 219; s. c., 7 Am. Rep. 513; Gay v. Minot, 3 Cush. 352.

[2] Freeman on Judgments, sec. 121.

[3] Griffith v. Frazier, 8 Cranch, 9; Flinn v. Chase, 4 Den. 90.

[4] Fisk v. Norvel, 9 Tex. 13; s. c., 58 Am. Dec. 128.

[5] Wales v. Willard, 2 Mass. 120.

then presented, the person interested in opposing it may regard it as abandoned. The court has no authority to hear it without giving a new notice.¹ But if the failure to present the application arises from the fact that the term of court is not opened, no presumption of abandonment can be indulged. The petition may, it has been held, be presented at the next term without any new notice.²

The complete exercise of jurisdiction over a subject-matter may exhaust the jurisdiction, not only of the court so exercising it, but of another court possessing concurrent jurisdiction over the same subject-matter. Thus, if in the progress of the administration of an estate in the probate court of a county, certain lands of a decedent are authorized to be, and are sold, the sale confirmed, and a conveyance made to the purchaser, the jurisdiction of the court over such lands is clearly exhausted. They become the property of the purchaser, and cannot again be subject to administration during the continuance of his life and ownership. If the district court of the county also possesses probate jurisdiction, and subsequently assumes authority over the estate of the decedent, and orders the same lands to be sold, and they are in fact sold to a purchaser having no knowledge of the former proceedings, such sale is void, because the former sale completely exhausted all probate jurisdiction over the lands, and the latter sale was a mere unauthorized assumption of authority over the property of a living person.³

§ 8. **General Principles Governing Jurisdictional Inquiries.**—In attempting to decide whether a judicial, execution, or probate sale can be avoided on the ground that the court entering the judgment or order of sale, did not have jurisdiction over the person of the defendant, the

---

¹ Turney v. Turney, 24 Ill. 625; Gibson v. Roll, 30 Ill. 172; Morris v. Hogle, 37 Ill. 150. See also Freeman on Judgments, sec. 526.
² Hanks v. Neal, 44 Miss. 224.
³ Lindsay v. Jaffray, 55 Tex. 626.

first inquiry will be to ascertain whether the court was a court of general jurisdiction, or a court of special or limited jurisdiction, or, in other words, whether it is a court of record, or one not of record. This inquiry must be conducted chiefly in the statutes of the State. If the court is a court of record, this jurisdictional question can, in most States, be decided with comparative ease. Courts of record are presumed to act correctly. When a court of record has entered judgment, its jurisdiction over the defendant is presumed, unless its record shows the contrary.[1] If, however, the record shows what was done toward acquiring jurisdiction, nothing else will be presumed to have been done.[2] An apparent exception to this rule is where the return on the summons shows an insufficient or void service, and the judgment or decree contains recitals or findings in favor of the jurisdiction of the court. In this case the recital or finding prevails. The court is presumed to have had other evidence than that contained in the return on the summons.[3] If the record shows that the court acquired jurisdiction of the defendant, or even if it is silent on that subject, jurisdiction will always be presumed.[4] In most States the presumption is conclusive, but in some a collateral attack may be made; and if, from such attack, it appears that the defendant was never brought before the court, the judgment will be held void.[5] In a majority of the States, if the proceeding is under some special statute, and in derogation of the common law, the jurisdictional presumptions in favor of a court of record, are not indulged. The inquiry must be conducted as though the court were not a court of record.[6] If the court is one not of record,

---

[1] Freeman on Judgments, sec. 124.

[2] Ib., sec. 125; Moore v. Starks, 1 Oh. St. 372; Benson v. Cilley, 8 Oh. St. 613.

[3] Freeman on Judgments, sec. 130.

[4] Ib., secs. 131, 132, 134.

[5] Ib., sec. 133.

[6] Ib., secs. 123, 127.

great care must be taken to see that every act essential to jurisdiction has been performed,[1] and performed in a proper manner.[2] No presumptions are indulged in favor of the jurisdiction of a court not of record. Its jurisdiction must always be shown affirmatively.[3] According to many of the authorities, it must be shown from the papers, files and proceedings in the case.[4] On the other hand, the fact that these show jurisdiction is not conclusive. They are not records importing absolute verity. They may be contradicted.[5] The courts having the administration of the estates of the deceased or of incompetent persons, are, in some States, of general, and in others of limited or special jurisdiction. Probably, in the majority of the States, they are of the latter class. Where this is the case, he who claims title under these courts must show affirmatively (and generally from their records and files) the taking of every step essential to jurisdiction.[6] Nothing will be presumed in his favor. But in several of the States these courts are either courts of record, or are, by statute, placed on the same footing as courts of record, with reference to jurisdiction, and are presumed to have acquired jurisdiction over all parties in interest, except where their records and proceedings indicate the contrary.[7]

The presumption in favor of jurisdiction may go further than merely rendering unnecessary the proof of the service

[1] Ib., sec. 517.
[2] Ib., sec. 521.
[3] Ib., secs., 517, 527.
[4] Ib., see. 518.
[5] Ib., sec. 517.
[6] Gwin v. McCarroll, 1 S. & M. 351; Rigney v. Coles, 6 Bosw. 479; Fell v. Young, 63 Ill. 106; Taylor v. Walker, 1 Heisk. 734; Gibbs v. Shaw, 17 Wis. 201; Root v. McFerrin, 37 Miss. 17.
[7] Doe v. Bowen, 8 Ind. 197; s. c., 65 Am. Dec. 758; Gerrard v. Johnson, 12 Ind. 636; Doe v. Harvey, 3 Ind. 104; Spaulding v. Baldwin, 31 Ind. 376; Valle v. Fleming, 19 Mo. 454; s. c., 61 Am. Dec. 566; Tucker v. Harris, 13 Ga. 1; s. c., 58 Am. Dec. 488; Brown v. Redwyn, 16 Ga. 76; Wood v. Crawford, 18 Ga. 526; Davie v. McDaniel, 47 Ga. 200; Jones v. Edwards, 78 Ky. 6.

of notice or of process. An inspection of the papers remaining among the files of the court may not be rewarded by the discovery of any petition for the sale, or may disclose the fact that some other essential writing is not to be found. Where the court is deemed to be one of general jurisdiction, the presumption is indulged that the missing document originally existed, and was sufficient in form, and that it has been lost from the files.[1] If a long period has elapsed between the date of a judicial or execution sale and the time when its validity is questioned, the presumption that the court and its officers did their duty is usually indulged, and the sale is upheld notwithstanding there is no direct or positive evidence of the existence of certain acts prescribed by law.[2]

ORDERS OF SALE IN PROBATE, AND HOW AUTHORITY TO MAKE MUST BE OBTAINED.

§ 9. Probate Sales without License of the Court; when Valid and when Void.—In execution and chancery sales, jurisdictional inquiries need to be prosecuted with much less care and frequency than in the consideration of sales made by executors, administrators or guardians. In a suit in equity, or an action at law, if the complaint discloses a cause which the court was competent to entertain and decide, and the record shows that jurisdiction was obtained over the persons of the defendants, it is generally safe to forego all further jurisdictional inquiries. But in probate proceedings, jurisdictional inquiries are material at almost every stage, and to be inattentive to them is to be guilty of rash imprudence. The application for letters testa-

---

[1] Doolittle v. Holton, 28 Vt. 819: s. c., 67 Am. Dec. 745; Hurley v. Barnard, 48 Tex. 83; Alexander's Heirs v. Maverick, 18 Tex. 179; s. c., 67 Am. Dec. 693.
[2] Seward v. Dideen, 16 Neb. 58; s. c., 20 N. W. Rep. 12; Whitman v. Fisher, 74 Ill. 147; Stevenson's Heirs v. McReary, 12 S. & M. 9; s. c., 51 Am. Dec. 102.

mentary, or of administration, the citation to the parties in interest, the hearing of the proofs and the order made thereon, correspond substantially to the complaint, the issue and service of process, and the trial and judgment at law. But here the case at law ends, while the case in probate is but scarcely commenced. What makes the probate proceeding still more perilous is, that a clear case of jurisdiction at this stage is not sufficient to support subsequent proceedings tending to divest the title of the heirs. At each subsequent stage, where the interest of the heir is sought to be affected, petitions and citations are usually exacted; and, in most courts, are treated as being jurisdictional in their nature. In some circumstances an executor, administrator, or guardian, may sell property without obtaining leave from the court. Where the statute has not adopted a different rule, " the whole personal estate of the testator or intestate rests in his executor or administrator;"[1] and "an executor or an administrator has an absolute power of disposal over the whole personal effects of the testator or intestate, and they cannot be followed by creditors, much less by legatees, either general or special, into the hands of an alienee. The principle is, that the executor or administrator, in many instances, must sell in order to perform his duty in paying debts, etc., and no one would deal with him if liable afterwards to be called to an account."[2] Where the common law rules upon the subject still prevail, a guardian, though not vested with any estate in the personal

---

[1] Lomax on Executors, (2d ed.) 367; Goodwin v. Jones, 3 Mass. 518; s. c., 3 Am. Dec. 173; Hayes v. Jackson, 6 Mass. 152; Sneed v. Hooper, Cooke, 200; s. c., 5 Am. Dec. 691; Petrie v. Clark, 11 S. & R. 377; s. c., 14 Am. Dec. 636, and note.

[2] Lomax on Executors, (2d ed.) 560; Overfield v. Bullitt, 1 Mo. 749; Williamson v. Branch Bank, 7 Ala. 906; Bland v. Muncaster, 24 Miss. 62; Nugent v. Gifford, 1 Atk. 463. An administrator may sell, without an order of court, a term of 999 years, for that is personalty (Petition of Gay, 5 Mass. 419); but not the estate of a mortgagee, for that is realty. *Ex parte* Blair, 13 Met. 126.

property of his ward, has an ample power of disposition over it.' "Though it be not in the ordinary course of the guardian's administration to sell the personal property of his ward, yet he has the legal right to do it, for it is entirely under his control and management, and he is not obliged to apply to court for direction in every particular case. The question as to the due exercise of the power arises between the guardian and his ward; and I apprehend that no doubt can be entertained as to the competency of the guardian's power over the disposition of the personal estate, including the choses in action, as between him and a *bona fide* purchaser." [1] So an executor might, at common law, and may, under the statutes of most of our States, sell real estate devised to him by the testator, or over which the will gives him a power of sale.[2] The power of a testator to authorize his executor to sell his real or personal estate without applying to court for permission, is generally conceded, though in some of the States such sales must be reported to and approved by the court.[3] The nomination of certain persons as executors, and investing them with power to sell the testator's real estate at their discretion, and without any license from the court, indicates that the testator has unusual confidence in the fidelity and sagacity of the persons so nominated and empowered. This unusual and somewhat irresponsible authority may, in the judgment of the testator, be safely and even advantageously conferred on the executors named in the will, but

---

[1] Field v. Schieffelin, 7 Johns. Ch. 153; s. c., 11 Am. Dec. 441; Tuttle v. Heavy, 59 Barb. 334; Tyler on Infancy and Coveture, 261-2; Thompson v. Boardman, 1 Vt. 367; s. c., 18 Am. Dec. 684; Truss v. Old, 6 Rand. 556; s. c., 18 Am. Dec. 748.

[2] 1 Lomax on Executors, (2d ed.) 384, 402, 560, and authorities in the next citation.

[3] Delaney's Estate, 49 Cal. 77; Jackson v. Williams, 50 Ga. 553; Durham's Estate, 49 Cal. 491; Crusoe v. Butler, 36 Miss. 170; Bartlett v. Sutherland, 24 Miss. 395; Going v. Emery, 16 Pick. 107; s. c., 26 Am. Dec. 645; Payne v. Payne, 18 Cal. 291; Larco v. Casaneuava, 30 Cal. 567; Cal. Code C. P., sec. 1561.

it is hardly probable that he would wish to see any other persons invested with it. Hence, where persons named as executors and invested with powers of sale have declined, or been unable to act, it has been held that the special confidence reposed in them by the will could not be vested in any other person, and that the administrator with the will annexed had no power to make sales, except by permission of the court.[1] That, in some cases, a power of sale, vested by the will in an executor, does not, in the event of his death, resignation or failure to qualify, vest in the administrator with the will annexed is established by a very decided preponderance of the authorities, and is, perhaps, not necessarily inconsistent with any of the cases. If the executor is merely invested with a discretion to sell if he thinks best so to do, this discretionary power cannot be exercised by an administrator with the will annexed.[2] If, on the other hand, executors be directed to sell, so that it would be impossible to accomplish the designs of their testator otherwise than by a sale, it is quite clear that he did not choose them for the purpose of having the benefit of their judgment in determining whether or not there should be any sale; and there seems to be no reason why his direction to sell may not be executed by part of his executors, if some of them fail to qualify, or, after qualifying, from any cause become incompetent to act,[3] or by an administrator with the will annexed, in case all the executors should resign or become disqualified or unable to

---

[1] Tippett v. Mize, 30 Tex. 361; Brown v. Hobson, 3 A. K. Marsh. 380; s. c., 13 Am. Dec. 187; Lockwood v. Stradley, 1 Del. Ch. 298; s. c., 12 Am. Dec. 97; Conklin v. Edgerton, 21 Wend. 430; Dunning v. Ocean Nat'l Bank, 61 N. Y. 497; s. c., 19 Am. Rep. 293; Cooke v. Platt, 98 N. Y. 35.

[2] See authorities in preceding citation.

[3] Taylor v. Galloway, 1 Oh. 232; s. c., 13 Am. Dec. 605; Zebach v. Smith, 3 Bin. 69; s. c., 5 Am. Dec. 352; Marr v. Peay, 2 Murph. 84; s. c., 5 Am. Dec. 521; Nelson v. Carrington, 4 Munf. 332; s. c., 6 Am. Dec. 519.

act.[1] Except where authorized to do so by a will, or by some statute, neither an administrator, an executor, nor a guardian can sell real estate without a license or order of sale from the court. A sale made without such license or order of court is not a mere error or irregularity which must be objected to by some proceeding in the court where the license ought to have been sought and granted; and, which, if not so objected to, is waived or ratified. It is a proceeding without any legal support. A conveyance made in pursuance of it has no force whatever. It may be shown to be void when collaterally attacked. In fact, no attack, collateral or otherwise, need be made.[2] The claimant under the sale could not show a *prima facie* case. In many of the States the power of guardians, executors and administrators over personal property does not extend to its transfer without leave of the court. An attempted transfer, made without such leave is, in such States, void.[3]

§ 10. **Petition for Order of Sale must be by a Person Competent to Present it.**—We now pass to the most numerous class of probate sales—those which must be sanctioned by a pre-existing order of court. This order must, in turn, be supported by certain pre-existing facts. In

---

[1] Peebles v. Watts' Admr., 9 Dana, 103; Kidwell v. Brummagim, 32 Cal. 438; Steele's Ex. v. Moxley, 9 Dana, 139; Gulley v. Prather, 7 Bush. 167; Gaines v. Fenter, 82 Mo. 497; Bailey v. Brown, 9 R. I. 79; Brown v. Armistead, 6 Rand. 594; Evans v. Chew, 71 Pa. St. 47; Mott v. Ackerman, 92 N. Y. 539.

[2] Tippett v. Mize, 30 Tex. 361; Beard v. Rowan, 1 McLean, 135; Robinson v. Martel, 11 Tex. 149; Low v. Purdy, 2 Lans. 422; Anderson v. Turner, 3 A. K. Marsh. 131; French v. Currier, 47 N. H. 88; Hite v. Taylor, 3 A. K. Marsh. 353; Goforth v. Longworth, 4 Oh. 129; s. c., 19 Am. Dec. 588; Jackson v. Todd, 1 Dutch. 121; Gelstrop v. Moore, 26 Miss. 206; s. c., 59 Am. Dec. 254; Bell's Appeal, 66 Pa. St. 498; Evans v. Snyder, 64 Mo. 516.

[3] Kendall v. Miller, 9 Cal. 591; De La Montagnie v. Union Ins. Co., 42 Cal. 291; Wells v. Chaffin, 60 Ga. 677. Where there is a valid order of sale, the sale of any parcel of land, in addition to the lands described in such order, is without any authority of law, and is, therefore, absolutely void. Burbank v. Semmes, 99 U. S. 138.

fact, the order of sale bears more resemblance to a judgment obtained in a new action, than to an order made in a pre-existing proceeding in which jurisdiction has already been acquired. To obtain an order of sale, a petition or complaint must be filed, a citation or notice must be issued and served, and a complete adversary proceeding conducted. Any jurisdictional defects in this proceeding are as fatal as if connected with the original grant of administration. And, what is worse, defects, which, in actions at law, would be treated as mere errors, are, in probate proceedings, counted as incurable jurisdictional infirmities. If a complaint in an action at law, or in a suit in equity, does not state facts sufficient to entitle the complainant to relief, its deficiency must be pointed out, or a judgment or decree is likely to be entered, which, though reversible on appeal, is valid until so reversed. If the complaint were filed by some one having no capacity to maintain the suit or action, that incapacity would be called to the attention of the court in some manner; or, if that were not done, a judgment would probably be entered in favor of plaintiff, and this judgment would not be void. But the presentation of a petition in probate by a person authorized to so petition, is a jurisdictional fact. If it be presented by some one not qualified to present it, there is no jurisdiction—no power to hear and determine it. If the court erroneously grants the prayer of the petition, there need be no appeal—the order is void and cannot support a sale.[1] In the case of two or more acting executors or administrators, a petition for an order of sale, preferred by any less than the whole, is irregular, but probably is not so worthless that the court can base no valid action upon it.[2] If the petition is by a

[1] Miller v. Miller, 10 Tex. 319; Washington v. McCaughan, 34 Miss. 301.

[2] Fitch v. Witbeck, 2 Barb. Ch. 161; Gregory v. McPherson, 13 Cal. 578; Downing v. Rugar, 21 Wend. 178; s. c., 34 Am. Dec. 223. See, as sustaining petitions by one administrator only, Jackson v. Robinson, 4 Wend. 437; De Bardelaben v. Stoudenmire, 48 Ala. 643.

person acting as administrator, but who has never qualified as such,[1] or is a special administrator not authorized by law to present the petition or make the sale,[2] or it appears from the whole record of the probate proceedings that his appointment was illegal, then the license and the sale based thereon are both void.[3]

The authority of a guardian or administrator, is confined to the State by whose courts he was appointed. Hence, he cannot be authorized to sell property situate in another State.[4] A sale made by a foreign guardian, or by a parent in his capacity of natural guardian,[5] or by one who falsely represents himself to be a guardian,[6] or by one who has ceased to be guardian,[7] is void. If the statute requires the application for a guardian's sale to be filed in the county in which the ward resides, or in case he resides out of the State, then in the county in which the land sought to be sold lies, the filing in the proper county has been held to be jurisdictional, and, therefore, a prerequisite to a valid order of sale.[8]

§ 11. **There must be a Sufficient Petition for License to Sell—What Petitions are Insufficient.**—As, in an action at law, the declaration should aver the facts entitling the plaintiff to judgment, so in a petition in probate, for authority to sell property, the matters necessary to justify the sale must be set forth. In truth, this necessity seems to be more imperative in the case of the petition than in that of the declaration. The judgment of a court of law

---

[1] Pryor v. Downey, 50 Cal. 389; s. c., 19 Am. Rep. 650.
[2] Long v. Burnett, 13 Ia. 28.
[3] Frederick v. Pacquette, 19 Wis. 541; Sitzman v. Pacquette, 13 Wis. 291; Chase v. Ross, 36 Wis. 267; Sumner v. Parker, 7 Mass. 79; Withers v. Patterson, 27 Tex. 501; Ex parte Barker, 2 Leigh. 719; Miller v. Jones 26 Ala. 247; Allen v. Kellam, 69 Ala. 442. See *ante*, sec. 2.
[4] McAnulty v. McClay, 16 Neb. 418; s. c., 19 N. W. Rep. 266.
[5] McNeil v. F. C. S., 4 W. C. Rep. 421.
[6] Grier's Appeal, 101 Pa. St. 412.
[7] Phelps v. Buck, 40 Ark. 219.
[8] Spellman v. Dow, 79 Ill. 66.

can rarely, if ever, be treated as void, because pronounced upon an insufficient complaint. An order in probate must be supported by a petition sufficient in substance to show a legal cause for the order. A license to sell, granted without any petition therefor, is void.[1] But a mere petition is not enough. The statutes of each State designate the contingencies in which the real estate of a deceased or incompetent person may be ordered to be sold. The probate courts have no power to license a sale in the absence of these contingencies. The statute prescribes the limit of the judicial authority. Action beyond this limit is not irregular or erroneous merely—it is non-judicial. If the causes of sale designated by statute are too few, relief must be sought from the legislature. An order of sale made to accomplish a purpose not sanctioned by statute, or based upon a necessity not recognized by statute, is, in legal effect, *coram non judice*. It cannot justify a sale made in pursuance of its directions.[2] The theory of the law is, that the probate courts have no general authority to dispose of the estate in process of administration; that their power of disposition is special and limited, and that he who relies upon the power must disclose a state of facts sufficient to call it into being. It is also essential that the petition state a sufficient cause of action. The order of the court is based upon the petition, and cannot draw its support from beyond the peti-

---

[1] Alabama Conference v. Price, 42 Ala. 39; Wyatt's Admr. v. Rambo, 29 Ala. 510; s. c., 68 Am. Dec. 89; Teverbaugh v. Hawkins, 82 Mo. 180; Ethell v. Nichols, 1 Idaho, (N. S.) 741; Finch v. Edmondson, 9 Tex. 504. But in Withers v. Patterson, 27 Tex. 499, and in Alexander v. Maverick, 18 Tex. 179, s. c., 67 Am. Dec. 695, it was intimated that the absence of a petition might not be fatal, and so decided in Rumrill v. St. A. Bank, 28 Minn. 202.

[2] Bompart v. Lucas, 21 Mo. 598; Farrar v. Dean, 24 Mo. 16; Newcomb v. Smith, 5 Oh. 448; Withers v. Patterson, 27 Tex. 499; Strouse v. Drennan, 41 Mo. 298; Beal v. Harmon, 38 Mo. 435; Ikelheimer v. Chapman, 32 Ala. 676; Sanford v. Granger, 12 Barb. 392; Woodruff v. Cook, 2 Edw. Ch. 259; Cornwall's Estate, 1 Tucker, 250; Hall v. Chapman, 35 Ala. 553.

tion, unless the statute otherwise provide. If the petition states no cause of sale, it would not be competent to prove, in support of the sale, that the court in fact received evidence of facts not relied upon by the petition, and that its action was, in fact, induced by proof of the causes of sale omitted from the petition but specified in the statute.[1] Some of the statutes designate, in general terms, the purposes for which a sale may be licensed, and declare that the application for such license must be in writing and must show the necessity for the sale. Other statutes enumerate with considerable particularity the matters to be inserted in the petition. Even where the statute does not contain any special enumeration of the matters to be stated, it is evident that a petition may be fatally defective: 1st, when it seeks an improper object; as, for instance, the sale of property for a supposed benefit to the estate, when the statute authorizes a sale for no such purpose; and, 2d, when a proper object is sought, but the sale is not shown to be necessary to obtain it, as where a sale is asked to pay debts, but no debts are shown to exist, or the deficiency of personal assets with which to pay the debts is not affirmed. "A long series of decisions in this State—uniformly holding to the same rule—has determined that the application of an executor or administrator for the sale of lands belonging to the estate is a special and independent proceeding; that the jurisdiction of the probate court depends absolutely on the sufficiency of the petition—in other words, on its substantial compliance with the requirements of the probate act. Though the proceeding for the sale occurs in the general course of administration, it is a distinct proceeding in the nature of an action, in which the petition is the commencement and the order of sale is the judgment. The necessity for a sale is not a matter for the administrator or executor to determine, but is a conclusion which the court must draw from the facts stated, and the petition must

[1] Pryor v. Downey, 50 Cal. 389; s. c., 19 Am. Rep. 656.

furnish materials for the judgment."¹ The policy of the law has always been in favor of preserving the real estate of heirs. Hence, if any necessity arises for the raising of money, resort must first be had to the personal estate of the heir or ward. It is not probable that a petition for the sale of real estate would give jurisdiction to any probate court in the Union, if it failed to show that the personal estate was either exhausted or was insufficient to produce the requisite funds.² By a statute of New York, an administrator, suspecting the personal estate of the deceased to be insufficient to pay the debts, was required to make an account of such personal estate and deliver it to the judge of the court of probate, or the surrogate of the county, and request his aid in the premises. Thereupon, an order issued to the persons interested, to show cause why the real estate should not be sold. The account, being essential to showing the deficiency of personal assets, was treated as jurisdictional. A sale, in its absence, was always held void.³ In most States the proceedings for the sale of real estate are adversary proceedings. In such proceedings parties defendant, as well as plaintiff, are essential. As the heirs occupy the position of defending parties, the petition should show who they are, in order that they may be

¹ Pryor v. Downey, 50 Cal. 398; s. c., 19 Am. Rep. 656; Haynes v. Meeks, 20 Cal. 288; Gregory v. McPherson, 13 Cal, 562; Hall v. Chapman, 35 Ala. 553; Jackson v. Robinson, 4 Wend. 436; Fitch v. Miller, 20 Cal. 352. But by section 1518 Code Civil Procedure of California, " a failure to set forth the facts showing the sale to be necessary will not invalidate the subsequent proceedings, if the defect be supplied by the proofs at the hearing, and the general facts showing the necessity be stated in the order directing the sale." See also sec. 1537, Cal. C. C. P.

² Gregory v. Tabor, 19 Cal. 397; Stuart v. Allen, 16 Cal. 473; s. c., 76 Am. Dec. —; Wattles v. Hyde, 9 Conn. 10.

³ Bloom v. Burdick, 1 Hill, 130; s. c., 37 Am. Dec. 299; Corwin v. Merritt, 3 Barb. 341; Ford v. Walsworth, 15 Wend. 450; Jackson v. Crawfords, 12 Wend. 533; Atkins v. Kinnan, 20 Wend. 241; s. c., 32 Am. Dec. 534; Wood v. McChesney, 40 Barb. 417. See Forbes v. Halsey, 26 N. Y. 53.

brought into court.¹ The failure to name them has been held fatal.² The petitioner cannot, at the hearing, abandon the grounds stated in his petition and obtain a license to sell on some other ground. A court having jurisdiction of a petition for a sale to pay debts, cannot thereon grant a valid license to sell to promote the interest of the heirs.³ The property sought to be sold must generally be described in the petition. No jurisdiction is obtained over that which is not described. A license to sell the whole of the real estate of a decedent, based on a petition to sell a part, is void.⁴ But a description will not be inadequate to support the order of sale, if it is such as would be sufficient in a conveyance, or as is rendered intelligible by the aid of facts of which the court has judicial knowledge.⁵ The petition need not state, in Missouri, that the property belonged to the decedent.⁶ In Kansas it does not appear to be essential to particularly describe the real property of a decedent in a petition for its sale. It is sufficient in that State, at least, when the question arises collaterally, that the petition aver that it is necessary to sell the real estate and name the county in which it is situate.⁷ This decision is not, in our judgment, sustained by the cases upon which the court appears to rely, and we apprehend it will find little favor in any court which regards itself as bound by the general rule

---

¹ Morris v. Hogle, 37 Ill. 150; Hoard v. Hoard, 41 Ala. 590; Turney v. Young, 22 Ill. 253.

² Guy v. Pierson, 21 Ind. 18. *Contra*, that the omission of the names of the heirs is an irregularity merely. Gibson v. Roll, 27 Ill. 92; Stow v. Kimball, 28 Ill. 106; Morris v. Hogle, 37 Ill. 150.

³ Williams v. Childress, 25 Miss. 78.

⁴ Verry v. McClellan, 6 Gray, 535; s. c., 66 Am. Dec. 423; Tenny v. Poor, 14 Gray, 502.

⁵ Smitha v. Flournoy, 47 Ala. 345. "Southeast quarter of sect. 19, T. 12:9" is fatally defective as a description. Weed v. Edmonds, 4 Ind. 468. "Section 12, T. 17, R. 21," was held sufficient in Wright v. Ware, 50 Ala. 549.

⁶ Trent v. Trent, 24 Mo. 307.

⁷ Bryan v. Bauder, 23 Kas. 95.

that a sale of real estate must be supported by a sufficient petition. If there is anything essential in a petition or complaint, we think it must be a designation of its subject-matter, in language sufficiently exact to enable a competent person to understand its location and extent. If real property is described as "the undivided one-half of a league of land on Clear Lake," or as "the undivided one-half part of a farm and vineyard at Sonoma, containing eight hundred and thirty-three acres, more or less," or as "eighty acres of land lying north of Courtland, and east of the Lamb's Ferry Road," it is clear that no person, from these descriptions alone, can locate the tracts thus imperfectly designated, and that sales based on such descriptions must be void.[1] Some of the more recent cases exhibit a disinclination to enforce the general rule exacting a sufficient petition as a prerequisite to a valid order of sale. The petitions sustained in such cases, will generally be found either to be deficient in formal matters, while they set forth informally matters amply adequate to sustain a sale, or else to be aided by some statute which undertakes to limit the cases in which sales of the class in question may be adjudged void.[2] But it is still requisite in most, if not in all of the States, that the action of the court be based on a sufficient petition; and by sufficient petition we mean one which at least shows the property intended to be sold, the existence of facts warranting such sale under the statutes of the State, and generally such other facts as the statute directs to be inserted in such petition, to enable the court the better to judge of the necessity or advisability of the sale.[3]

---

[1] Wilson v. Hastings, 5 W. C. Rep. 31; Gilchrist v. Shackleford, 72 Ala. 7.

[2] McKeever v. Ball, 71 Ind. 398; Worthington v. Dunkin, 41 Ind. 515; Moffit v. Moffit, 69 Ill. 641; Stanley v. Noble, 59 Ia. 666.

[3] Boland's Estate, 55 Cal. 310; Wilson v. Hastings, 5 W. C. Rep. 31; Rose's Estate, 63 Cal. 346; Wright v. Edwards, 10 Org. 298; Hayes v. McNealy, 16 Fla. 409; Ryder v. Flanders, 30 Mich. 336; Young v. Young, 12 Lea. 335; Arnett v. Bailey, 60 Ala. 435.

There are other matters with respect to which the provisions of the statute have been regarded as directory merely. Thus, though the statute directs that the petition shall be verified, the absence of such verification has never been held fatal.. The jurisdiction of the court was thought to be called into action by a petition stating the requisite facts, and the absence of verification was adjudged to be a mere irregularity.[1] An administrator or executor, in petitioning for a sale, need not aver the death of the testator or intestate, nor the time or mode of the petitioner's appointment; but may simply, upon this subject, state that he is the executor or administrator, as the case may be, of the decedent.[2]

§ 12. **Statutes Designating what Petition for Order of Sale must Contain.**—Where a statute enumerates the matter to be contained in the petition for the sale of real estate, its object is to compel petitioners to disclose the supposed necessity of the sale, and also to furnish information which will aid the court in determining upon the best course of action, in case it finds a sale to be necessary. The statute of California exacts more than any other which has come under our observation.[3] It requires a verified petition setting forth: 1, the amount of personal property that has come into the hands of the administrator, and how much remains undisposed of; 2, the debts of the decedent; 3, the amount due or to become due on the family allowance; 4, the debts, expenses and charges of administration accrued and to accrue; 5, a general description of all the real property of which the decedent died seized, or in which he had any interest, or in which the estate has acquired any

---

[1] Ellsworth v. Hall, 48 Mich. 407; s. c., 12 N. W. Rep. 512; Coon v. Fry, 6 Mich. 506; Trumble v. Williams, 24 N. W. Rep. 716; Johnson v. Jones, 2 Neb. 126; Williamson v. Warren, 55 Miss. 199.

[2] Moffatt v. Moffat, 69 Ill. 641; Stow v. Kimball, 28 Ill. 93.

[3] C. C. P. of Cal., sec. 1537. See also Hurd's Stat. of Ill., pp. 121, 123; Dassler's Stat. of Kans., sec. 2027; Comp. Laws Mich. 1871, p. 1424, sec. 4546; 1 Biss. Stat. of Minn., p. 673, sec. 178; Wag. Stat. Mo., pp. 94, 96, secs. 10, 25.

interest, and the condition and value thereof, and whether the same be community or separate property; 6, the names of the heirs, legatees and devisees of the deceased, so far as known to the petitioner. If any of the matters here enumerated cannot be ascertained, it must be so stated in the petition.[1] Whenever the question has arisen, the supreme court of this State has decided that the power of the probate court to order a sale depended upon a petition in substantial compliance with the statute.[2] In Missouri, if any person die and his personal estate be insufficient to pay his debts and legacies, his executor or administrator shall present a petition stating the facts.[3] The petition shall be accompanied by a true account of his administration; a list of debts due to and by the decedent, and remaining unpaid, and an inventory of the real and personal property, with its appraised value, and all other assets.[4] It seems now to be settled in that State, that the jurisdiction of the court attaches on the filing of the petition, and that the omission of the accounts and lists, required by statute to accompany it, is not fatal.[5] In Wisconsin and several other States, the statute provides that sales shall not be avoided on account of any irregularity, if it appears: 1, that the executor, administrator or guardian was licensed to make the sale by the probate court having jurisdiction; 2, that he gave a bond on the granting of the license; 3,

---

[1] C. C. P. of Cal., sec. 1537.

[2] Gregory v. McPherson, 13 Cal. 562; Stuart v. Allen, 16 Cal. 473; s. c., 76 Am. Dec. —; Townsend v. Gorden, 19 Cal. 188; Gregory v. Taber, 19 Cal. 397; Haynes v. Meeks, 20 Cal. 288; Fitch v. Miller. 20 Cal. 352; also, to same effect, Ackley v. Dygert, 33 Barb. 190; Bree v. Bree, 51 Ill. 367.

[3] 1 Wag. Stat. of Mo., p. 94, secs. 10, 11.

[4] 1 Wag. Stat. of Mo., p. 94, sec. 22.

[5] Overton v. Johnson, 17 Mo. 442; Mount v. Valle, 19 Mo. 621; Grayson v. Weddle, 63 Mo. 523; Pattee v. Thomas, 58 Mo. 163. These cases, we think, are, in principle, directly opposed to the New York cases—Bloom v. Burdick, 1 Hill, 130; s. c., 37 Am. Dec. 299; Ford v. Walsworth, 15 Wend. 450; Jackson v. Crawfords. 12 Wend. 533.

that he took the oath as prescribed by statute before making the sale; 4, that he gave the notice of the sale; and, 5, that the premises were sold in good faith and the sale confirmed. Under this statute, sales based on defective petitions are held valid.[1]

§ 13. **Petitions for Sale Liberally Construed—When other Papers may be Referred to.**—The rule of law that declares void probate sales based on insufficient petitions, is very harsh in its operation. To avoid the necessity of applying the rule, the courts will construe petitions as liberally as possible. They will not require the use of the exact language of the statute; they will forgive all errors of form; they will regard it as sufficient if the matters stated are substantially those required to be stated; and, in interpreting the language used, they will seek to find in it something to support, rather than to destroy the title based on the probate proceedings.[2] In drafting the petition, reference may be had to some other paper on file, and, by such reference, this paper may be made a part of the petition. The petition, for instance, may state that a full description of the real and personal estate can be ascertained from the inventory on file. Where this is done, it will be sufficient that this jurisdictional fact appears from the inventory.[3] But, to justify a reference to the inventory or other paper on file, " it must have been referred to in the petition, so as to become a part of it, for the purpose of refer-

---

[1] Reynolds v. Schmidt, 20 Wis. 374; Mohr v. Tulip, 40 Wis. 66; Mohr v. Manierre, 9 C. L. N. 270; 1 Biss. Stat. Minn., p. 680, sec. 223; Coon v. Fry, 6 Mich. 506; Woods v. Monroe, 17 Mich. 238; McKeever v. Ball, 71 Ind. 406; Runwell v. St. Albans Bank, 28 Minn. 202.

[2] Morrow v. Weed, 4 Ia. 77; s. c., 66 Am. Dec. 122; King v. Kent's Heir's, 29 Ala. 542; Moffit v. Moffit, 69 Ill. 641; De Bardelaben v. Stoundenmire, 48 Ala. 643; Fitch v. Miller, 20 Cal. 382; Haynes v. Meeks, 20 Cal. 315; Wright v. Ware, 50 Ala. 549; Maurr v. Parrish, 26 Oh. St. 636; Wing v. Dodge, 80 Ill. 564; Bowen v. Bond, 80 Ill. 351.

[3] Bentz's Est., 36 Cal. 687; Stuart v. Allen, 16 Cal. 501; s. c., 76 Am. Dec. —; Sheldon v. Wright, 7 Barb. 47.

ence;"[1] and it seems that the reference made to the inventory or other paper on file, must designate the imperfection or defect which it was intended to supply. Thus, where the reference to the inventory purports to be "for greater certainty," "without stating for what the reference was made, whether for description, or value, or condition," the court said: "We think this reference was insufficient to incorporate the inventory as a part of the petition as to description, or value, or condition."[2] In this case the inventory mentioned several pieces of real property, some of which were sufficiently and others insufficiently described. The statute required the description of all the lands of the decedent, in any petition for their sale. The object of this requisition was to disclose to the court all the real property of the decedent, to aid in determining the necessity for the sale of the whole or any part of the lands, and if of a part only, then to advise the court as to which part. Hence, it was held that the fact that some of the parcels were sufficiently described, does not, even as to these parcels, cure the defect arising from the imperfect description of the other parcels.[3]

§ 14. **Petition need not be True.**—The jurisdiction of the court over the subject-matter attaches on the filing of a petition sufficient in form. The matter stated in the petition may or may not be true. The functions of the court are of such a character that it may inquire into the truth or falsity of the petition. The petition may be regarded as a complaint. The heirs, when jurisdiction over them is obtained, may be treated as entering a general denial. The order of the court, granting or refusing the prayer of the petition, is in the nature of a judgment conclusively establishing that the sale is or is not necessary. If erroneous, it must be corrected by appeal, or some other appropriate

---

[1] Gregory v. Taber, 19 Cal. 409.
[2] Wilson v. Hastings, 5 W. C. Rep. 31.
[3] Ibid.

proceeding. It cannot be collaterally avoided by showing that the petition was false.[1]

§ 15. **Cases Holding that no Notice is Necessary.**—We have already spoken of the proceeding in probate to obtain a sale of real estate, as an independent, adversary proceeding *in personam*. If it be, in fact, such a proceeding, then the defendants must be brought before the court by something which is equivalent to the service of process, and given an opportunity of resisting, in case they deem resistance proper to be made. Nearly all the statutes require some order to show cause against the petition, to issue and to be served on the parties in interest, either personally or by publication. In a few of the States this requirement is not jurisdictional. The purchaser need not, in those States, ask whether the notice to show cause against the petition was or was not given. The sale is valid if supported by a sufficient petition and an order of sale made thereon. "On a proceeding to sell the real estate of an indebted estate, there are no adversary parties, the proceeding is *in rem*, the administrator represents the land; they are analagous to proceedings in the admiralty, where the only question of jurisdiction is the power of the court over the thing—the subject-matter before them—without regard to the persons who may have an interest in it; all the world are parties. In the orphan's court, and all courts who have power to sell the estates of intestates, their action operates on the estate, not on the heirs of the estate; a purchaser claims, not their title, but one paramount. The estate passes to him by operation of law. The sale is a proceeding *in rem*, to which all claiming under the intestate are parties."[2]

---

[1] Jackson v. Crawfords, 12 Wend. 533; Fitch v. Miller, 20 Cal. 382; Stuart v. Allen, 16 Cal. 473; s. c., 76 Am. Dec. —; Haynes v. Meeks, 20 Cal. 288; McCauley v. Harvey, 49 Cal. 497; Grignon's Lessee v. Astor, 2 How. U. S. 339; Bowen v. Bond, 80 Ill. 351; Grayson v. Weddle, 63 Mo. 523.

[2] Grignon's Lessee v. Astor, 2 How. U. S. 338; Beauregard v. New Orleans, 18 How. U. S. 497; Comstock v. Crawford, 3 Wall. 396; Tongue

This position is maintained more frequently with respect to guardian's sales, than with respect to those made by executors or administrators, and with more plausibility. For the petition for sale filed by a guardian, it is with much force insisted, is merely the petition of the ward acting through his duly accredited agent. Under this view, the ward is, in legal effect, the petitioner, and there is no necessity of advising him of the existence of his own petition, and warning him that it will, at a certain time, be granted. If any notice is required by statute, it is claimed that such notice is for the protection of third persons whose interests may somehow be affected; and that its omission in nowise impairs the force of the proceedings as against the ward.[1]

§ 16. **Notice of Petition—Cases Holding it Indispensable.**—A very decided majority of the authorities is opposed to the principles stated in the preceding section. This majority declares that the proceeding, to obtain an order to sell real estate, is a new and independent proceeding *in personam*, in which the petitioner is the plaintiff, the petition is the complaint, the parties whose property is to be sold are the defendants, and the order to show cause, or the notice to appear is the summons; that the defendants are not in court until this summons is served, or its service has

---

v. Morton, 6 H. & J. 21; McPherson v. Cundiff, 11 S. & R. 422; s. c., 14 Am. Dec. 642; Gager v. Henry, 5 Saw. C. C. 237; Doe v. McLoskey, 1 Ala. 708; Perkins v. Winter, 7 Ala. 855; Matheson v. Hearin, 29 Ala. 210; Duval's Heirs v. P. and M. Bank, 10 Ala. 636; Field's Heirs v. Goldsby, 28 Ala. 224; Satcher v. Satcher's Adm'r, 41 Ala. 39; Rogers v. Wilson, 13 Ark. 507; Sheldon v. Newton, 3 Oh. St. 494; George v. Watson, 19 Tex. 354; Mohr v. Manierre, 101 U. S. 41; 9 Ch. L. N. 270; Ewing v. Higby, 7 Oh. St. 1, p. 198; Robb v. Irwin, 15 Oh. 689; Snevely v. Lowe, 18 Oh. 368; Benson v. Cilley, 8 Oh. St. 614—overruling Adams v. Jeffries, 12 Oh. 272.

[1] Mohr v. Porter, 51 Wis. 487; Mohr v. Manierre, 101 U. S. 41; s. c., 9 Ch. L. N. 270; Mulford v. Beveridge, 78 Ill. 458; Spring v. Kane, 86 Ill. 580; Montgomery v. Johnson, 34 Ark. 74.

been waived by persons competent to waive it; and that whenever it is conceded or shown that any person interested was not summoned to appear, substantially as provided by statute, the whole proceeding, as against him, is utterly void.[1] The administrator, as such, has no control over the real estate left by the intestate. His authority to sell, if it exists, was conferred by the orders of the surrogate and the other proceedings before him. The latter derives his power from the statutes, and in order to confer the authority upon the administrator to transfer the title to the land, and thus disinherit the heirs of the intestate, it is requisite that the directions of the statute, so far as they relate to the acquiring of jurisdiction of the subject-matter, and of the parties to be affected by the proceedings, should be strictly complied with. These principles are elementary, and no citation of authority to sustain them is necessary.[2]

§ 17. **The Service of Notice on a Minor cannot be Waived nor Dispensed with.**—It cannot be waived by the minor, because he is incompetent to act for himself.[3] Neither can it be waived by a guardian, unless the statute

---

[1] Halleck v. Moss, 17 Cal. 339; Coy v. Downie, 14 Fla. 544; Clark v. Thompson, 47 Ill. 25; Doe v. Bowen, 8 Ind. 197; s. c., 65 Am. Dec. 758; Gerrard v. Thompson, 12 Ind. 636; Babbitt v. Doe, 4 Ind. 355; Good v. Norley, 28 Ia. 188; Washburn v. Carmichael, 32 Ia. 475; Valle v. Fleming, 19 Mo. 454; s. c., 61 Am. Dec. 596; Campbell v. Brown, 6 How. (Miss.) 106; Winston v. McLendon, 43 Miss. 554; Puckett v. McDonald, 6 How. (Miss.) 269; Vick v. Mayor, 1 How. (Miss.) 379; s. c., 31 Am. Dec. 169; Hamilton v. Lockhart, 41 Miss. 460; French v. Hoyt, 6 N. H. 370; s. c., 25 Am. Dec. 464; Corwin v. Merritt 3 Barb. 341; Schneider v. McFarland, 2 N. Y. 459; Dakin v. Hudson, 6 Cow. 222; Fiske v. Kellogg, 3 Org. 503; Taylor v. Walker, 1 Heisk. 734; Gibbs v. Shaw, 17 Wis. 197; Blodgett v. Hitt, 29 Wis. 169; Beckett v. Selover, 7 Cal. 215; s. c., 68 Am. Dec. 237; Rankin v. Miller, 43 Ia. 11; Mickel v. Hicks, 19 Kas. 578; s. c., 27 Am. Rep. 161; Rule v. Broach, 58 Miss. 552; Wisner v. Brown, 50 Mich. 553; Pinckney v. Smith, 26 Hun. 524; Bloom v. Burdick, 1 Hill, 130; s. c., 37 Am. Dec. 299.

[2] Sibley v. Waffle, 16 N. Y. 185.

[3] Winston v. McLendon, 43 Miss. 254.

in direct terms invests him with that power.[1] Nor can the court by any means exonerate itself from complying with the statute. It cannot, without service of the notice on the minor, appoint any guardian *ad litem* for him. The appointment of such guardian and his subsequent appearance in the cause as the representative of the minor cannot cure any jurisdictional defect, nor tend to the validation of a proceeding otherwise void.[2] Service of notice on the guardian of a minor does not, in the absence of a statute to that effect, dispense with the necessity for serving the minor himself.[3] In New York, a guardian must be appointed for minor heirs on filing the petition, and notice must thereafter be given to heirs. The giving of the notice, in advance of the appointment of the guardian, is invalid.[4] If the person applying for the license to sell is also the guardian of the minors, his position as petitioner is incompatible with his duty as guardian. He cannot, therefore, represent the heir, and the latter must have another representative appointed for the occasion.[5] In Indiana, the statute authorizes the guardian of a minor, on the presentation of a petition for the sale of lands in which he is interested, to appear for him and consent to the sale. This was held to confer authority upon a person, filling the offices of administrator and guardian, to petition for a sale in his former capacity, and to assent to it in the latter.[6] In Illinois, proceedings by a guardian for the sale of the lands of his ward are purely *in rem*.[7] In Florida, no service of

---

[1] Doe v. Anderson, 5 Ind. 33.

[2] Chambers v. Jones, 72 Ill. 275; Moore v. Starks, 1 Oh. St. 369; Good v. Norley, 28 Ia. 188; Clark v. Thompson, 47 Ill. 25.

[3] Clark v. Thompson, 47 Ill. 25.

[4] Ackley v. Dygert, 33 Barb. 176; Havens v. Sherman, 42 Barb. 636; Schneider v. McFarland, 2 N. Y. 459.

[5] Havens v. Sherman, 42 Barb. 636; Schneider v. McFarland, 2 N. Y. 459; Townsend v. Tallant, 33 Cal. 52; Kennedy v. Gaines, 51 Miss. 625.

[6] Jones v. Levi, 72 Ind. 586.

[7] Mulford v. Beveridge, 78 Ill. 455.

process on an infant heir is required. The court must appoint a guardian *ad litem*. But if no guardian *ad litem* is appointed, and the general guardian is served with process and appears and represents the minor, the proceedings are not void.[1] In Mississippi, if the guardian of a minor petitions for the sale of the lands of his ward, no notice need be given the latter. A summons must issue to the co-heirs, and also to three of the nearest relatives of the minor living in the State. The omission to summon these relatives is fatal to the subsequent proceedings.[2]

§ 18. **The Notice Must be Given in the Manner Prescribed by Statute, or it is Inoperative.**[3]—If it attempts a description of the land sought to be sold, the description must be correct. A license to sell one tract of land, founded on a notice, designating a different tract is void.[4] If a statute direct notice to be given by personal service, unless publication thereof is ordered by the court, a publication is, in the absence of such order, inoperative.[5] If a copy of the petition and account are required to be served, the service of a summons in their stead is unauthorized and, therefore, void.[6] If a publication is directed to be made in a specified newspaper for four weeks, it cannot be made in that paper for three weeks, and in another paper the remaining week.[7] If the return day named in the order to show cause, though fixed by the court, is not a day on which it can by law be made returnable,[8] or is not sufficiently distant to permit the giving of the notice for the full time

---

[1] Price v. Winter, 15 Fla. 66.

[2] Stampley v. King, 51 Miss. 728.

[3] Herdman v. Short, 18 Ill. 59; Gibson v. Roll, 27 Ill. 190; Morris v. Hogle, 37 Ill. 150; Schnell v. Chicago, 38 Ill. 383; Bree v. Bree, 51 Ill. 367.

[4] Frazier v. Steenrod, 7 Ia. 339; s. c., 71 Am. Dec. 417. *Contra* Maurr v. Parrish, 26 Oh. St. 636.

[5] Halleck v. Moss, 17 Cal. 339.

[6] Johnson v. Johnson, 30 Ill. 223.

[7] Townsend v. Tallant, 33 Cal. 45.

[8] Haws v. Clark, 37 Ia. 355.

prescribed by law, the subsequent proceedings based on such order to show cause are void.¹ Ordinarily, there is a wide distinction between the effect of process defectively served and process not served at all; and this distinction, to some extent at least, applies to proceedings in probate. Hence, it has been held that, under a statute requiring the notice of application for an order of sale to be personally served on a minor, a return showing service by reading the notice to the minor and leaving a copy with his father, is sufficient to maintain the jurisdiction of the court over such minor, because the case " is not one of no notice, but of defective service of notice." ²

§ 19. **The Notice Must be Given for the Time Prescribed.**—The publication of a notice for a shorter time than that sanctioned by law is void, and can impart no validity to a sale or other subsequent proceeding resting upon it.³ This is true, although the time is shortened by an order of court in a case where the statute does not give the court that power.⁴ If a statute requires the notice to be published for three successive weeks, the first publication to be six weeks before the presentation of the petition, and the notice, as published, designates a day for the presentation less than six weeks from the date of the first publication, the notice is void, and cannot be made valid by presenting the petition at a later day than that specified in the notice.⁵ No notice need be given to persons in adverse possession, unless the statute directs it.⁶ Giving notice to a person acting in one capacity seems not to affect him when claiming in another capacity. Hence, a consent given

---

¹ Stilwell v. Swarthout, 81 N. Y. 109.
² Bunce v. Bunce, 59 Ia. 532.
³ Townsend v. Tallant, 33 Cal. 45; Corwin v. Merritt, 3 Barb. 341; Monahan v. Vandyke, 27 Ill. 155; Havens v. Sherman 42 Barb. 636. *Contra*, by statute, Woods v. Monroe, 17 Mich. 245.
⁴ Havens v. Sherman, 42 Barb. 636.
⁵ Gibson v. Roll, 30 Ill. 178.
⁶ Yeomans v. Brown, 8 Met. 51.

by a woman as guardian of minors was held not to prejudice her claim as widow of the decedent.[1]

§ 20 The Order of Sale and Its Effect as an Adjudication.—If, upon hearing of the petition, the court is satisfied that a proper case exists, it will enter an order or license for the sale of the land. If the court had jurisdiction, this order, until vacated or reversed, is binding upon all parties in interest. The purchaser under it is in no danger of losing his title by proof being made that the order was erroneously given. It cannot be collaterally attacked for error, fraud or irregularity, if the court had jurisdiction.[2] When jurisdiction is once obtained over a proceeding, the decision of the court is always conclusive on the parties which it keeps within the limits of its jurisdiction, unless reversed upon appeal, or by some other proceeding sanctioned by law for the purpose of correcting errors of proceeding or decision. This rule applies to courts of inferior, limited or special jurisdiction, as well as to those of the highest rank and most comprehensive authority. When a court grants an order of sale, and in pursuance of such order the property thereby authorized to be sold is sold, the purchaser, to maintain his title, is not required to re-establish the facts which the court must have found to be true before it entered such order, nor yet to defend the legal conclusions which the court drew from such facts. If any errors were committed, as in the admission or rejection of evidence, or in making findings of

[1] Helms v. Love, 41 Ind. 210.

[2] Freeman on Judgments, sec. 319a; Stow v. Kimball, 28 Ill. 93; Beckett v. Selover, 7 Cal. 215; s. c., 68 Am. Dec. 237; Farrington v. King, 1 Bradf. 182; Spragins v. Taylor, 48 Ala. 520; Jackson v. Robinson, 4 Wend. 437; Boyd v. Blankman, 29 Cal. 19; Myer v. McDougal, 47 Ill. 278; Carter v. Waugh, 42 Ala. 452; Morrow v. Weed, 4 Ia. 77; s. c., 66 Am. Dec. 122; Atkins v. Kinnan, 20 Wend. 241; s. c., 32 Am. Dec. 534; Mulford v. Stalzenback, 46 Ill. 303; Savage v. Benham, 17 Ala. 119; Sprigg's Estate, 20 Cal. 121; Giddings v. Steele, 28 Tex. 750; Gurney's Succession, 14 La. An. 622; Hatcher v. Clifton, 33 Ala. 301; Walker v. Morris, 14 Ga. 323; Barbee v. Perkins, 23 La. An. 331; Gordon v. Gordon, 55 N. H. 399.

fact, express or implied, not warranted by the evidence, or in reaching conclusions not warranted by the facts found, the remedy of any party prejudiced thereby was by motion for new trial, or by some other revisory or appellate proceeding. Failing to resort to this remedy, the order of sale must be respected, and cannot be destroyed by any collateral assault.[1] Hence, the sale cannot be nullified by proof that there was no necessity therefor, nor by any other proof which involves a re-examination of the issues necessarily involved in the order of sale.[2] There are some cases which appear to permit a re-examination of the legal conclusions drawn by the court in ordering the sale. Thus, sales were held void in one instance, because ordered to raise funds to pay debts barred by the statute of limitation,[3] and in another because the order did not show any necessity for the sale.[4] If these and kindred cases can be maintained upon principle, it must be on the ground that the petitions and orders were so deficient in essential elements that they did not disclose any case calling for judicial action, and, therefore, left the court without jurisdiction, according to the decisions cited in section eleven.

The form of the order is different in the different States. In California, it "must describe the lands to be sold and the terms of the sale."[5] In Massachusetts, it need not designate which part of the testator's lands are to be sold.[6] In Texas, an order to sell all the lands of a decedent

---

[1] Myers v. Davis, 47 Ia. 325; Fleming v. Bale, 23 Kans. 88; McDade v. Burch, 7 Ga. 559; s. c., 50 Am. Dec. 407; Long v. Weller, 29 Gratt. 347; Grayson v. Weddle, 63 Mo. 523; Pratt v. Houghtating, 45 Mich. 457; Weyer v. Second Nat'l Bank, 57 Ind. 198; Gardner v. Mawney, 95 Ill. 552; Merrill v. Harris, 26 N. H. 143; s. c., 57 Am. Dec. 359.

[2] Bowen v. Bond, 80 Ill. 351; Allen v. Shepard, 87 Ill. 314; Myers v. Davis, 47 Ia. 325; Arrowsmith v. Harmoning, 42 Oh. St. 254; Davis v. Gaines, 104 U. S. 386; Abbott v. Curran, 98 N. Y. 665; Cromwell v. Hull, 97 N. Y. 209.

[3] Heath v. Wells, 5 Pick. 139; s. c., 16 Am. Dec. 383.

[4] Wyatts v. Rambo, 29 Ala. 510; s. c., 68 Am. Dec. 89.

[5] C. C. P. of Cal., sec. 1551.

[6] Yeomans v. Brown, 8 Met. 51; Norton v. Norton, 5 Cush. 524.

was thought to be proper,[1] while a license for the sale of so much as would raise $1,500 (it appearing that the decedent held 34,000 acres) was regarded as of very questionable validity.[2] In Alabama, a license to sell must designate the place of sale.[3] In Texas, the direction of the statute that the order of sale contains a description of the property to be sold was held to be directory merely.[4] In Georgia, the order may be to sell "all the real estate of the decedent," without any further attempt at description.[5] In Arkansas, the fact that the order contains no description does not render it inoperative, if it appears to be granted on a certain petition and that petition contains a full and adequate description.[6] In California, "the order of sale must be in itself sufficient; and to make it so, the description of land to be sold must be sufficiently definite and certain, without reference to any extraneous matter."[7] Hence, the description "twenty-one acres of the Ranch La Golita, being the share of a tract of thirty-one acres allotted to said minors by a decree of the district court of Santa Barbara county, in a suit in partition wherein the guardian herein and mother of said minors was plaintiff and said minors were defendants," is fatally defective. Giving the number of the lot and block without naming the village or city is insufficient,[8] but land may be described by abreviations in common use, as "Sec. 12, T. 17, R. 21," if the county is named;[9] and the mentioning of "ninety-one acres of the southwest corner" of a designated tract, where the decedent owned only that number of acres in such tract, was held to be sufficient.[10]

[1] Wells v. Polk, 36 Tex. 120.
[2] Graham v. Hawkins, 38 Tex. 628.
[3] Brown v. Brown, 41 Ala. 215.
[4] Robertson v. Johnson, 57 Tex. 62.
[5] Doe v. Henderson, 4 Ga. 148; s. c., 48 Am. Dec. 216.
[6] Montgomery v. Johnson, 31 Ark. 74.
[7] Hill v. Wall, 4 W. C. Rep. 503; Crosby v. Dowd, 61 Cal. 557.
[8] Herrick v. Ammerman, 21 N. W. Rep. 836.
[9] Wright v. Ware, 50 Ala. 549; Money v. Turnipseed, 50 Ala. 499.
[10] Bloom v. Burdick, 1 Hill, 130; s. c., 37 Am. Dec. 299.

CHAPTER III.

SALES VOID BECAUSE OF ERRORS OR OMISSIONS SUBSEQUENT TO THE JUDGMENT OR ORDER OF SALE.

SECTION.
21. General Rule Regarding the Effect of Irregularities.
22. Failure to give Additional Bond, or to take Oath Concerning the Sale.
23. The Necessity of a Valid Execution, or Order of Sale.
24. The Times when an Execution may not Issue.
25. Writs of Execution must be Sufficient in Form.
26. Sales in the Absence of Levies.
27. Sales without Inquisition or Appraisement.
28. Sales without Notice.
29. Sales, by Whom may be Made.
30. Sales made at an Improper Time.
31. Sales made at an Improper Place.
32. Sales not at Public Auction.
33. Sales to Persons Disqualified from Purchasing.
34. Sales to Raise More Money than was Authorized.
35. Sales of Property not Liable to Sale.
36. Sale of Different or Less Interest.
37. Sale of Unlocated Part.
38. Sales of Property in Adverse Possession.
39. Sales *en masse*.
40. Sales Infected by Fraudulent Combinations and Devices.
41. Purchaser's Title not Affected by Secret Frauds.

§ 21. **General Rule Regarding Irregularities.**—When a judgment or order of sale has been pronounced, it must next be enforced. The authority which pronounces it is judicial. That which enforces it is chiefly ministerial. In the exercise of this ministerial authority, various errors of commission or of omission are likely to occur. We shall devote this chapter to a brief and, necessarily, imperfect enumeration of those ministerial errors, on account of which a judicial, execution or probate sale may be adjudged void. With respect to judicial and execution sales, "the general principle to be deduced from the authorities is, that the title of a purchaser, not himself in fault, cannot be impaired at law nor in equity by showing any mere error or irregularity in the proceedings. Errors and irregularities must be corrected by a direct proceeding. If not so corrected, they cannot be made available by way of collateral attack on the purchaser's title."[1] Probate sales, we are sorry to say, are generally viewed with extreme suspicion. Though absolutely essential to the administration of justice, and forming a portion of almost every chain of title, they are too often subjected to tests far more trying than those applied to other judicial sales. Mere irregularities of proceeding have, even after the proceedings had been formally approved by the court, often resulted in the overthrow of the purchaser's title. In fact, in some courts, the spirit manifested toward probate sales has been scarcely less hostile than that which has made tax sales the most precarious of all of the methods of acquiring title. In other courts, however, probate sales are treated as indulgently as other judicial sales.[2] It is sometimes said that a

---

[1] Freeman on Executions, sec. 339; Freeman on Cotenancy and Partition, sec. 548; Winchester v. Winchester, 1 Head, 460; Whitman v. Taylor, 60 Mo. 127; Hedges v. Mace, 72 Ill. 472; Cooley v. Wilson, 42 Ia. 428; DeForest v. Farley, 62 N. Y. 628; Byers v. Fowler, 12 Ark. 218; s. c., 54 Am. Dec. 271; Sydnor v. Roberts, 13 Tex. 598; s. c., 65 Am. Dec. 84; Millis v. Lombard, 19 N. W. Rep. 187; Wallace v. Loomis, 97 U. S. 146; Fitzpatrick v. Peabody, 51 Vt. 195; Casey v. Gregory, 13 B. Mon. 505; s. c., 56 Am. Dec. 581; Walker v. McKnight, 15 B. Mon. 467; s. c., 61 Am. Dec. 190.

[2] Harris v. Lester, 80 Ill. 307; Price v. Winter, 15 Fla. 66; Mulford v. Beveridge, 78 Ill. 455; Patterson v. Lemon, 50 Ga. 231; Gage v. Schroder, 73 Ill. 44; Spring v. Kane, 86 Ill. 580; Goodbody v. Goodbody, 95 Ill. 456; Moody v. Butler, 63 Tex. 210.

sale made under a decree must pursue the directions therein contained, that a departure from these directions renders the sale void.[1] But to invoke this rule, the departure must be of a very material character; and must, we think, be a departure which has not been approved by a decree of confirmation entered in the court which ordered and had supervision of the sale.[2]

§ 22. **Failure to Give Additional Bond, or to Take Oath Concerning the Sale.**—The granting of a license to sell real estate imposes a duty and also a pecuniary responsibility on the guardian or administrator, in addition to the duty and responsibility otherwise attached to his office. This duty is to use his best efforts to make an advantageous sale of the property. This responsibility is to properly account for and pay over the proceeds of the sale. To insure a greater fidelity in performing this duty, some statutes have prescribed an oath to be taken before entering upon any of the proceedings necessary to precede the sale. To provide against any misappropriation of the proceeds of the sale, the statutes very generally exact an additional bond from the guardian, executor or administrator. The fact that a sale was made, or that the time or place thereof was selected in advance of the taking of this oath, has, in every case coming within our observation, been decided to be fatal to the purchaser's title.[3] The same conclusion has been reached in several cases where sales were made without the giving of the additional bond.[4] In most of the cases

---

[1] Williamson v. Berry, 8 How. (U. S.) 544; Jarboe v. Colvin, 4 Bush. 70; Cofer v. Miller, 7 Bush. 545.

[2] Welch v. Louis, 31 Ill. 446; McGavock v. Bell, 3 Caldw. 512.

[3] Campbell v. Knights, 26 Me. 224; s. c., 45 Am. Dec. 107; Wilkinson v. Filby, 24 Wis. 441; Parker v. Nichols, 7 Pick. 111; Blackman v. Bauman, 22 Wis. 611; Williams v. Reed, 5 Pick. 480; Cooper v. Sunderland, 3 Ia. 114; s. c., 66 Am. Dec. 52; Thornton v. Mulquinne, 12 Ia. 549.

[4] Wiley v. White, 3 Stew. & P. 355; Currie v. Stewart, 26 Miss. 646; Babcock v. Cobb, 11 Minn. 347; Rucker v. Dyer, 44 Miss. 591; Perkins v. Fairfield, 11 Mass. 226; Cohea v. State, 34 Miss. 179; Hamilton v. Lockhart, 41 Miss. 460; Washington v. McCaughan, 34 Miss. 304; Wil-

where sales were held void for the failure to take the oath or to give the bond, they had been confirmed by the court. In Indiana and Pennsylvania, the failure to file the additional bond is an irregularity merely. After the confirmation and the payment of the money, this failure cannot avoid the sale.[1] In New York, the filing of the original bond, on the granting of letters of administration, is not a jurisdictional matter.[2] The issue of letters without it is valid. The failure of a master in chancery to file his bond, cannot be raised in a collateral suit to avoid a sale made by him and confirmed by the court.[3]

In Indiana, a sale made without giving the bond required, cannot be avoided collaterally when made by a guardian, if he has duly accounted for the proceeds. If, on the other hand, such proceeds have been lost to the ward, owing to the omission of the bond, he may treat the sale as void.[4] It thus appears to be the duty of the purchaser in that State either to assure himself that the requisite bond has been given, or else to take measures looking to the proper application of the proceeds of the sale. In some of the States the legislature has, by statute, declared that probate sales shall not be avoided on account of "any irregularity in the proceedings, provided it should appear: 1, that the executor was licensed to make the sale by the county court having jurisdiction; 2, that he gave a bond that was approved by the judge of the county court, in case a bond was required, upon granting a license; 3, that he took the oath therein prescribed; 4, that he gave notice of the time and place of sale as therein prescribed; and, 5, that the

---

liams v. Morton, 38 Me. 47; s. c., 61 Am. Dec. 229; Williamson v. Williamson, 3 S. & M. 715; s. c., 41 Am. Dec. 636. For application of a similar rule in partition suits, see Freeman on Cotenancy and Partition, sec. 466.

[1] Foster v. Birch, 14 Ind. 445; Lockhart v. John, 7 Pa. St. 137.
[2] Bloom v. Burdick, 1 Hill, 130; s. c., 37 Am. Dec. 299.
[3] Nicholl v. Nicholl, 8 Pai. 349.
[4] McKeever v. Ball, 71 Ind. 398.

premises were sold accordingly, and the sale confirmed by the court, and that they were held by one who purchased them in good faith."[1] These statutes, while professedly in the interest of purchasers in good faith at probate sales, probably operate to the contrary, as they seem to recognize five classes of irregularity as fatal, when only the first of the five was clearly and necessarily fatal, independent of such statute. In States controlled by these or similar statutes, we see no escape from the conclusion that a sale, made in the absence of the bond required by law, or the order of the court, is void. But, unless supported by some statute, the decisions declaring that the failure to give such bond nullifies the sale, are not sustainable at all. The jurisdiction of the court is in nowise connected with the giving of the bond; and the omission of such bond is manifestly a simple irregularity affording sufficient reason for refusing to approve the sale, but of no consequence to a purchaser in good faith, except in so far as it may lead the court to withhold its approval of his purchase.[2]

§ 23. **The Necessity for a Valid Execution.**—Though a judgment at law be entered, no officer has any authority to enforce it without a writ of execution. A sale, when no such writ had issued, would, unquestionably, be void. In chancery, the decree of sale may of itself constitute a sufficient authority for its own execution.[3] The usual custom in chancery is to deliver a certified copy of the decree to the person charged by the court or by law with the duty of making the sale. Under the practice for the foreclosure of mortgages in California, the sheriff is authorized to proceed on receiving an execution or a certified copy of the decree.

---

[1] Melms v. Pfister, 59 Wis. 194.
[2] Wyman v. Campbell, 6 Porter, 319; s. c., 31 Am. Dec. 677; Palmer v. Oakley, 2 Doug. (Mich.) 433; s. c., 47 Am. Dec. 41; Bunce v. Bunce, 59 Ia. 533; Watts v. Cook, 24 Kans. 278; Mobberly v. Johnson, 78 Ky. 273; McKinney v. Jones, 55 Wis. 39.
[3] Karnes v. Harper, 48 Ill. 527.

If he acts in the absence of both, his acts are void.[1] Some of the statutes require copies of orders of sale in probate to be delivered to the administrator or guardian as his authority to sell, and others contain no direct provision on the subject. We have never known of a sale being questioned on the ground that no copy of the license to sell had been delivered to the administrator. An execution is invalid and cannot support a sale, unless it is issued out of a court,[2] and by an officer[3] competent to issue it. It must also be on a judgment capable of enforcement by execution. The judgment must not be void nor satisfied.[4] The defendant in execution must also be a person or corporation against which an execution may issue.[5] The execution must not be forged, either wholly nor in any material part.[6]

§ 24. **The Times When Execution May Not Issue.**—By some statutes a plaintiff's right to execution does not exist immediately after the entry of the judgment, but remains in abeyance a specified period of time. The issue of execution before the expiration of this time is, in most States, a mere irregularity, not of sufficient gravity to render the

---

[1] Heyman v. Babcock, 30 Cal. 367.

[2] Freeman on Executions, sec. 15. After a court has been abolished, an execution purporting to be issued out of it is a nullity. Harris v. Corriell, 80 Ill. 54.

[3] Freeman on Executions, sec. 23.

[4] Ib., secs. 19 and 20. That a sale under a satisfied judgment is void, is affirmed in French v. Edwards, 5 Saw. C. C. 266; Drefall v. Tuttle, 42 Ia. 77; Finley v. Gant, 8 Baxter, 148: Wood v. Colvin, 2 Hill, 566; s. c., 38 Am. Dec. 588; Frost v. Yonker's S. B., 70 N. Y. 560; Doe v. Ingersoll, 11 S. & M. 249; s. c., 49 Am. Dec. 57; Murrell v. Roberts, 11 Ired. 424; s. c., 53 Am. Dec. 449. In some States, such sales are upheld in favor of innocent purchasers. Van Campen v. Snyder, 3 How. (Miss.) 66; s. c., 32 Am. Dec. 311; Hoffman v. Strohecker, 7 Watts, 86; s. c., 32 Am. Dec. 740; Reed v. Austin, 9 Mo. 722; s. c., 45 Am. Dec. 336; Boren v. McGeehee, 6 Porter, 432; s. c., 31 Am. Dec. 695. A purchaser buying at a sale under a satisfied judgment, with notice of facts sufficient to put him upon inquiry, unquestionably gets no title. Kezar v. Elkins, 52 Vt. 119; Weston v. Clark, 37 Mo. 573.

[5] Freeman on Executions, sec. 22.

[6] Ib., secs. 23, 47; Silvan v. Coffee, 20 Tex. 4; s. c., 70 Am. Dec. 371.

sale void.¹ The same rule is usually applied to writs issued contrary to agreement or pending a stay of execution. They will be vacated on motion. But if the defendant takes no steps to obtain their vacation, or to set aside sales made thereunder, the latter will be treated as valid.² This remark is equally true of writs issued and sales made in disobedience of injunctions.³ At common law, execution could not regularly issue after a year and a day subsequent to the entry of judgment, without a revivor by *scire facias*. A writ issued in violation of this rule is not void.⁴ So, at common law, an execution could not regularly issue without revivor of the judgment by *scire facias*, after the death of a sole plaintiff or of a sole defendant. The issue of a writ, in violation of this rule, is a more serious matter than its issue on a dormant judgment. If an execution is issued and tested after the death of a sole plaintiff, the authorities are very evenly divided upon the question whether it is void or irregular only.⁵ But if it issues and bears *teste*, after the death of a sole defendant, the authorities almost, but not quite unanimously, adjudge it void.⁶ But the death of one of several plaintiffs or defendants neither suspends nor destroys the right to issue execution.⁷

---

¹ Freeman on Executions, sec. 25; Stewart v. Stocker, 13 S. & R.. 199; s. c., 15 Am. Dec. 589. But in Massachusetts a premature writ is void. Penniman v. Cole, 8 Met. 496.

² Freeman on Executions, secs. 26, 33; Swiggart v. Harber, 4 Beam. 364; s. c., 39 Am. Dec. 418.

³ Rikeman v. Kohn, 48 Ga. 183; Bagley v. Ward, 37 Cal. 121.

⁴ Freeman on Executions, secs. 29, 30; Riddle v. Turner, 52 Tex. 145. *Contra*, Godbold v. Lambert, 8 Rich. Eq. 155; s. c., 70 Am. Dec. 192; Hoskins v. Helm, 4 Litt. 309; s. c., 14 Am. Dec. 133.

⁵ Freeman on Executions, sec. 35.

⁶ Ib., sec. 35: Clingman v. Hophie, 78 Ill. 152; Welch v. Rattern, 47 Ia. 147; Collier's Admr. v. Windham, 27 Ala. 291; s. c., 62 Am. Dec. 767. In other cases writs so issued were adjudged to be voidable only, and not void. Shelton v. Hamilton, 23 Miss. 496; s. c., 57 Am. Dec. 149; Harrington v. O'Reilly, 9 S. & M. 216; s. c., 48 Am. Dec. 704.

⁷ Freeman on Executions, sec. 36. With respect to the effect of the death of a party after the issue of execution, see ib., sec. 37.

If an execution issue after a judgment is pronounced and before its entry by the clerk, the writ is not void. If necessary to maintain proceedings taken under the writ, the court would doubtless order the entry of the judgment *nunc pro tunc*.[1] If, however, the writ issues in anticipation of a judgment not yet ordered by the court, or upon a judgment of confession not yet perfected by the clerk, a more serious question arises. In such a case the writ, at the time of its issue and until the judgment is pronounced or perfected, is unquestionably void; and it seems that no validity can be infused into the writ by the subsequent rendition of the judgment.[2] In some of the States, executions may be issued by the clerk of a superior court upon transcripts of judgments of justices of the peace. The substantial performance of the various acts designated by statute, with respect to the transcript and the filing thereof, appear to be essential to the issuing of the writ and the maintainance of titles founded upon it.[3] The issue of a *venditioni exponas* when a *fieri facias* was ordered is a nullity. "The clerk has no power to issue any other writ than that prescribed in the judgment."[4]

§ 25. **Writs of Execution Must be Sufficient in Form.**—The necessity for a writ of execution cannot be answered by a writ, called by that name, but substantially defective in form. It must at least purport to proceed from some competent authority; must show what judgment it is designed to enforce, and must direct the officer to execute or satisfy the judgment.[5] But there are various formal matters usually embodied in writs of execution, and in respect of which an error or omission is not necessarily fatal. Thus, a mistake or omission in designating the

[1] Graham v. Lynn, 4 B. Mon. 17; s. c., 39 Am. Dec. 493.
[2] Hathaway v. Howell, 54 N. Y., 97; s. c., on second trial, 6 Thomp. & C., 453; 4 Hun. 270.
[3] Bigelow v. Booth, 39 Mich. 622.
[4] Hurst v. Liford, 11 Heisk. 622.
[5] Freeman on Executions, secs. 39-41.

return day,[1] or in the attesting clause,[2] are not of sufficient consequence to defeat an execution sale. In some courts an execution, without a seal (where one is required) is void; in others it is irregular merely.[3] The most frequent mistakes in the issue of writs are made in attempting to describe judgments. The name of the plaintiff or of the defendant may be incorrectly stated, or the amount of the judgment may vary from the sum for which execution issues. These mistakes and variances are amendable. If no amendment is made, and no objection to the form of the writ is interposed by a motion to quash or vacate it, it must be treated as valid, unless the variance is so great that it appears not to be issued upon the judgment which is produced in its support.[4] An execution not issued in the name of the people of the State, nor directed to the sheriff, is amendable, and a sale thereunder is valid.[5]

§ 26. **Sales in the Absence of Levies.**—When a judicial sale is made by virtue of an order or license of sale, no levy is necessary. The same rule holds good with respect to execution sales of real estate, where the judgment itself is a lien on the real property of the defendant. Personal property must be levied upon, or in some way subjected to the control of the officer, before a valid sale can be made under execution. As between the parties, the defendant can waive a levy. With respect to real estate, upon which

---

[1] Freeman on Executions, sec. 44; Brevard v. Jones, 50 Ala. 221; Youngblood v. Cunningham, 38 Ark. 571.
[2] Freeman on Executions, sec. 45; Douglas v. Haberstro, 88 N. Y. 611; Ross v. Luther, 4 Cow. 158; s. c., 15 Am. Dec. 341.
[3] Freeman on Executions, sec. 46; Roseman v. Miller, 84 Ill. 297; Taylor v. Taylor, 83 N. C. 116; Woolford v. Dugan, 2 Ark. 131; s. c., 35 Am. Dec. 52. and note.
[4] Freeman on Executions, secs. 42, 43; Harlan v. Harlan, 14 Lea, 107; Haskins v. Wallet, 63 Tex. 213; Alexander v. Miller's Ex., 18 Tex. 893; s. c., 70 Am. Dec. 314; Wilson v. Campbell, 33 Ala. 249; s. c., 70 Am. Dec. 586.
[5] Hibberd v. Smith, 50 Cal. 511.

a levy has neither been made nor waived, the authorities are very evenly divided as to the validity of an execution sale, some claiming that it is irregular merely, others that it is void.[1]

§ 27. **Sales Without Inquisition or Appraisement.**— Some statutes require an inquisition or appraisment of real estate to precede its sale under execution, and seek to avoid the great sacrifice sometimes attending compulsory sales by forbidding any sale which does not realize a certain proportion of the appraised value. Sales made without any appraisment, or for a less proportion of the appraised value than authorized by law, are usually, but not universally, held void.[2] In many of the States, administrators and guardians are required to have property appraised before selling it. In Missouri and Louisiana, sales made in contravention of these statutes are thought to be void;[3] but we apprehend that they should be declared voidable merely; and, if confirmed by the court, as entirely valid.[4]

§ 28. **Sales Void for Want of Notice of Sale.**—Some notice of the time and place of sale, and of the property to be sold, is obviously essential to the realization of its value. This notice is commonly required to be given by the statutes regulating judicial, execution and probate sales. Whether a compliance with this requirement is a prerequisite to the power to sell, is uncertain. Undoubtedly a sale, without first giving the proper notice, would not be confirmed if the defect were known to the court. It would be vacated

---

[1] Freeman on Executions, sec. 274; Gordon v. Gilfoil, 99 U. S. 168; Bledsoe v. Willingham, 62 Ga. 550; Wood v. Augustine, 61 Mo. 46; Elliott v. Knott, 14 Md. 121; s. c., 74 Am. Dec. —.

[2] Freeman on Executions, secs. 284, 285; Maple v. Nelson, 31 Ia. 322; Brown v. Butters, 40 Ia. 544. A sale under a forged waiver of inquisition is void. Zuver v. Clark, 104 Pa. St. 222.

[3] Strouse v. Drennan, 41 Mo. 298; Curley's Succession, 18 La. An. 728. But a sale in probate to pay debts is not void in Louisiana, because for less than the appraisement. Stoltz's Succession, 28 La. An. 175; Herrman v. Fontelieu, 29 La. An. 502.

[4] Bell v. Green, 38 Ark. 78.

on motion, while the court has power to annul it by that kind of proceeding.[1] Concerning execution sales, "a very decided preponderance of the authorities maintains this proposition: That the statutes requiring notice of the sale to be given are directory merely, and that the failure to give such notice cannot avoid the sale against any purchaser not himself in fault."[2] With respect to executors', administrators' and guardians' sales, the authorities are more evenly divided. On the one hand, they maintain that the giving of notice for the time, and substantially in the manner directed by statute, is indispensable to a valid sale.[3] On the other hand, they insist that the existence of the notice and its sufficiency are legitimate subjects of inquiry, when the sale is reported for confirmation, but not afterwards.[4]

There seems to be more reason for sustaining probate sales, made upon insufficient notice or without any notice whatever, than for sustaining sales so made upon execution, because the latter are not usually brought before the court

---

[1] Glenn v. Wootten, 3 Md. Ch. 514; Matter of McFeely, 2 Redf. 511; Helmer v. Rehm, 14 Neb. 219; Reynolds v. Wilson, 15 Ill. 394; s. c., 60 Am. Dec. 753.

[2] Freeman on Executions, sec. 286; Ware v. Bradford, 2 Ala. 676; s. c., 36 Am. Dec. 427; Brooks v. Rooney, 11 Ga. 423; s. c., 56 Am. Dec. 430; Solomon v. Peters, 37 Ga. 255; Howard v. North, 5 Tex. 290; s. c., 51 Am. Dec. 769; Draper v. Bryson, 17 Mo. 71; s. c., 57 Am. Dec. 257; Minor v. Natchez, 4 S. & M. 602; s. c., 43 Am. Dec. 488; Burton v. Spiers, 92 N. C. 503; Maddox v. Sullivan, 2 Rich. Eq. 4; s. c., 44 Am. Dec. 231, and note; Smith v. Randall, 6 Cal. 47; s. c., 65 Am. Dec. 475. *Contra*, Hughes v. Watt, 26 Ark. 228; Lafferty v. Conn, 3 Sneed, 221; Herrick v. Ammerman, 32 Minn. 544; Prater v. McDonough, 7 Lea, 670; Henderson v. Hays, 41 N. J. L. 387.

[3] Thomas v. Le Baron, 8 Met. 363; Curley's Succession, 18 La. An. 728; Blodgett v. Hitt, 29 Wis. 169; Mountour v. Purdy, 11 Minn. 384; Gernon v. Bestick, 15 La. An. 697; Hobart v. Upton, 2 Saw. C. C. 302.

[4] Morrow v. Weed, 4 Ia. 77; s. c., 66 Am. Dec. 122; Little v. Sinnett, 7 Ia. 324; Minor v. Selectmen, 4 S. & M. 602; Bland v. Muncaster, 24 Miss. 62; s. c., 57 Am. Dec. 162; Hanks v. Neal, 41 Miss. 212; McNair v. Hunt, 5 Mo. 301; Cooley v. Wilson, 42 Ia. 428; Hudgens v. Jackson, 51 Ala. 514; Moffit v. Moffit, 69 Ill. 641.

for confirmation, while the former are reported to and considered by the court, and are not to be approved unless the proceedings are fair and regular. To attack a probate sale after confirmation, for the purpose of showing the absence of or defects in the notice, involves the re-examination of an issue which has been once heard and determined by a court of competent jurisdiction, and the re-examination of which ought therefore to be forbidden.

§ 29. **By Whom the Sale May be Made.**—When a sale is to be made under a decree in chancery, the court may appoint some one as its agent or commissioner and invest him with power to make the sale.[1] A sale under execution must be made by a sheriff or constable, unless he is disqualified to act. So an administrator's sale must be made by or under the direction of the administrator. The court cannot appoint some other person to make the sale.[2] Nor can an executor appoint some person in his stead to exercise a power of sale contained in the will.[3] An administrator's or commissioner's sale, at which he was not present, and conducted by his agent, is voidable, if not void.[4] It seems to always be essential that the person making a sale in an official capacity be at least an officer *de facto*, and as such authorized to act in the particular case. A sheriff or constable has no authority to act under a writ directed to another sheriff or constable, and a sale made by him is void.[5] So a sale made by an ex-sheriff, in a case where the sheriff in office ought to have acted,[6] or by the sheriff in office where the ex-sheriff ought to have acted,[7] is without author-

[1] Freeman on Executions, sec. 291.
[2] Crouch v. Eveleth, 12 Mass. 503; Swan v. Wheeler, 4 Day, 137; Jarvis v. Russick, 12 Mo. 63; Rose v. Newman, 26 Tex. 131; State v. Founts, 89 Ind. 313.
[3] Pearson v. Jamison, 1 McLean, 197.
[4] Chambers v. Jones, 72 Ill. 275; Sebastian v. Johnson, 72 Ill. 282.
[5] Bybee v. Ashby, 2 Gilm. 151; s. c., 43 Am. Dec. 47; Gordon v. Camp, 3 Pa. St. 349; s. c., 45 Am. Dec. 647.
[6] Bank of Tenn. v. Beatty, 3 Sneed, 305; s. c., 65 Am. Dec. 58.
[7] Purl v. Duvall, 5 H. & J. 69; s. c., 9 Am. Dec. 490.

ity of law and void. The division of a county after the
levy on an execution does not devest the sheriff levying the
writ of power to make the sale.¹ A sheriff is incompetent
to execute a writ to which he is a party. A sale made by
him under a judgment in his favor is a nullity.² The rule
pronouncing sales void when conduced by officers having no
authority to make them, may operate harshly in some
instances, but it is justified by on the ground that the officer
is known not to be acting for himself, but as an agent, and
that it is always the duty of a person, dealing with one who
assumes to act as an agent, to ascertain, at his peril, the
existence of the latter's authority.

§ 30. **At What Time a Sale May be Made.**—Of course
no judicial or execution sale ought to take place at any
other time than that fixed by the notice of sale; and the
notice of sale ought not to fix upon any time prohibited by
law. A sale made in violation of this rule will, no doubt,
be vacated or refused confirmation if the irregularity is
suggested to the court at the proper time. It is not, however, void in most States.³ In Texas, a sale made at a time
different from that allowed by law cannot be collaterally
attacked after its confirmation.⁴ But if the irregularity be
not thus cured by confirmation, the sale is void.⁵ It is
always essential that a sale be made under a valid, subsisting authority. A sale made when such authority had been
destroyed by lapse of time would everywhere be treated as
void. If the statute, under which a license to sell is granted,
limits the operation of the license within a designated
period, a sale outside of the prescribed limit is a nul-

---

[1] Lofland v. Ewing, 5 Litt. 42; s. c., 15 Am. Dec. 41.
[2] Collais v. McLeod, 8 Ired. 221; s. c., 49 Am. Dec. 376; Bowen v. Jones, 13 Ired. 25.
[3] Freeman on Executions, sec. 287. *Contra*, Mayers v. Carter, 87 N. C. 146.
[4] Brown v. Christie, 27 Tex. 75.
[5] Peters v. Caton, 6 Tex. 556; Tippett v. Mize, 30 Tex. 365; Howard v. North, 5 Tex. 290; s. c., 51 Am. Dec. 769.

lity.¹ In some instances licenses to sell have been held to have lost their vitality through lapse of time, although the statute had not directly prescribed any such limit to their power.² If the act under which an order of sale has been granted is repealed, or the court in which it was entered is abolished, its legal vitality is destroyed, and it cannot support a subsequent sale.³ An execution cannot be legally levied after the return day thereof, and if a levy is attempted after such return day and is followed by a sale, both the levy and sale are void.⁴ But, by the common law, the levy of an execution creates a special property in the sheriff, and by virtue of such property he may proceed to sell after the return day of the writ, as well as before. This is unquestionably true with respect to personal property. A levy on real estate, however, creates no special property therein, and great contrariety of opinion has developed concerning the power of officers to make sales thereof after the return day of writs on levies made before such time. The weight of the authorities favors the validity of such sales.⁵

§ 31. **Sales Made at an Improper Place** are sometimes held to be irregular merely, but more frequently are adjudged void.⁶ Execution sales of real estate must be made

---

¹ Macy v. Raymond, 9 Pick. 285; Marr v. Boothby, 19 Me. 150; Mason v. Ham, 36 Me. 573; Williamson v. Williamson, 52 Miss. 725.

² Wellman v. Lawrence, 15 Mass. 326. In this case the sale was made fifteen years subsequent to the license.

³ McLaughlin v. Janney, 6 Gratt. 609; Perry v. Clarkson, 16 Oh. 571; Bank v. Dudley, 2 Pet. 493.

⁴ Jefferson v. Curry, 71 Mo. 85; Logsdon v. Spevey, 54 Ill. 104.

⁵ Freeman on Executions, sec. 106; Blair v. Compton, 33 Mich. 414; Wyant v. Tuthill, 17 Neb. 495; s. c., 23 N. W. Rep. 342; Johnson v. Bemis, 7 Neb. 224; Kane v. McCown, 55 Mo. 181; Phillips v. Dana, 3 Scam. 551; Pettingill, v. Moss, 3 Minn. 222; s. c., 74 Am. Dec. 747; note to Young v. Smith, 76 Am. Dec. 81. *Contra*, Sheppard v. Rhea, 49 Ala. 125; Paine v. Hoskins, 3 Lea, 284; Smith v. Mundy, 18 Ala. 182; s. c., 52 Am. Dec. 221; Rogers v. Cawood, 1 Swan. 143; s. c., 55 Am. Dec. 739; Mitchell v. Ireland, 54 Tex. 301; Williamson v. Williamson, 52 Miss. 725.

⁶ Freeman on Executions, sec. 289; Murphy v. Hill, 77 Ind. 129.

in the county where it is situate, and by an officer of such county;[1] but a commissioner in chancery may be authorized to sell real estate beyond the limits of the county in which he was appointed.[2] Personal property, capable of being examined and inspected, must, if possible, be at or near the place of sale. Bidders must be permitted to view it, and, by the exercise of their various senses, to judge of its character and value. Any other rule would tend to a wanton sacrifice of the property. Hence, a sale of personal property, at a place where it cannot be examined or seen, is a nullity.[3]

§ 32. **Sales Not at Public Auction.**—Execution sales must be made at public auction. Probate and other judicial sales are generally controlled, in this respect, by the directions contained in the license or decree. Whenever, by law or by direction in an order of sale, property is required to be sold at public auction, a private sale thereof is invalid.[4] There are cases which seem to sustain the view that an execution sale cannot be made, unless there are bidders or by-standers present other than the officers conducting the sale and the parties to the suit; and that a sale made to the judgment creditor, when there is no one present but himself and the sheriff, is a nullity.[5] The decision was placed upon

---

[1] Freeman on Executions, sec. 289; Morrell v. Ingle, 23 Kans. 32; Menges v. Oyster, 4 W. & S. 20; s. c., 39 Am. Dec. 50; Thacker v. Devol, 50 Ind. 30.

[2] Bank v. Trapier, 2 Hill Ch. 25.

[3] Freeman on Executions, sec. 290; Collins v. Montgomery, 2 N. & McC. 39; Kennedy v. Clayton, 29 Ark. 270. *Contra*, where valid levy has been made; Eads v. Stephens, 63 Mo. 90. And in Alabama, an execution sale of goods not present thereat, is voidable only. Foster v. Mabe, 4 Ala. 402; s. c., 37 Am. Dec. 749.

[4] Hutchinson v. Cassidy, 46 Mo. 431; Ellet v. Paxson, 2 W. & S. 418; Fambro v. Gantt, 12 Ala. 298; Wier v. Davis, 4 Ala. 442; McArthur v. Carrie, 32 Ala. 75; Gaines v. De La Croix, 6 Wall. 719; Neal v. Patterson, 40 Ga. 363; Ashurst v. Ashurst, 15 Ala. 781; Worten v. Howard, 2 S. & M. 527. *Contra*, Wynns v. Alexander, 2 D. & B. Eq. 58; Tynell v. Morris, 1 D. & B. Eq. 559.

[5] Ricketts v. Ungangst, 15 Pa. St. 90; s. c., 53 Am. Dec. 572; Michael v. McDermott, 17 Pa. St. 353; s. c., 55 Am. Dec. 560.

the ground that the presumption of collusion between the purchaser and officer was "irresistable and conclusive." If there were any circumstances tending to show that no sufficient notice of the sale was given, or that anything was done to prevent intending purchasers from attending the sale, then, in the event of plaintiffs purchasing, and especially if the purchase was for a decidedly inadequate sum, there might be sufficient reason, in the interest of sound public policy, for presuming a collusion and permitting this presumed collusion to vitiate the sale. But we know of no means by which the plaintiff in execution, or the officer conducting the sale, can compel the attendance of either of bystanders or of competing bidders, and are, therefore, unable to concur in the opinion that a sale in their absence is irresistable or conclusive evidence of collusion, or is any adequate ground for pronouncing such sale void, though we concede that, in the event of a gross inadequacy in the sum bid, or of any suspicious circumstances whatever, the fact that the sale took place without the presence of bidders or by-standers might well justify a court in setting it aside.

It has been held that the bid must be made at the time of the sale; that if the officer, receiving an offer of a designated sum before the sale, at the sale accepts and cries such offer, and makes a sale in pursuance of such offer, that the sale is void.[1] This decision is best justified on the ground that the bid in question being made and accepted in the absence of the bidder, could only be made through the instrumentality of the officer acting on behalf of the bidder, and that the law does not permit the officer to act as the agent of the purchaser.

§ 33. **Sales to Persons Disqualified From Purchasing.**—The policy of the law is not to permit the same person to represent conflicting interests. Hence, trustees, sheriffs, constables, administrators, executors, guardians,

---

[1] Sparling v. Todd, 27 Oh. St. 521.

and all persons vested with authority to sell the property of others, are themselves forbidden from becoming interested in the sale. A sale made in violation of this rule will always be vacated upon a motion made in due time.[1] But the only question strictly within the scope of our present inquiry is the effect of such a sale when no action is taken for the purpose of setting it aside. If the sale and conveyance be made directly to the administrator, sheriff or other officer, it may well be declared a nullity, on the ground that one person cannot unite in himself the capacity of vendor and vendee—cannot, by the same act, transmit and receive.[2] Two or more administrators or executors of the same decedent are, in law, treated as one person. Hence, even where the statute permits such an officer to purchase the property of the estate which he represents, one of them cannot convey to the other.[3] But usually laws are sought to be evaded rather than openly violated. Hence, an administrator or sheriff, desirous of becoming the owner of property about to be sold by himself, will seek the aid of a friend, in whose name the purchase can be made and the title held, for such time as will conceal the true nature of the transaction. In a case of this kind, the officer cannot be permitted to profit by the transaction at the expense and against the will of the parties interested. On learning the true state of the facts they may have the sale annulled, or they may affirm it and permit it to stand. If they seek to annul it, they are entitled to succeed, irrespective of the fairness or unfairness of the sale, or the motives which prompted the administrator or other officer or trustee.[4] But

---

[1] Freeman on Executions, sec. 292.
[2] Humblin v. Warnecke, 31 Tex. 91; Boyd v. Blankman, 29 Cal. 31; Stapp v. Toler, 3 Bibb. 450; Dwight v. Blackmar, 2 Mich. 330; s. c., 57 Am. Dec. 130.
[3] Green v. Holt, 76 Mo. 677.
[4] Riddle v. Roll, 24 Oh. St. 572; Anderson v. Green, 46 Ga. 361; Potter v. Smith, 36 Ind. 231; Smith v. Drake, 23 N. J. Eq. 302; Froneberger v. Lewis, 70 N. C. 456; Ryden v. Jones, 1 Hawks, 497; s. c., 9 Am. Dec.

the sale is not void in the extreme sense. It cannot be attacked and overthrown by third persons. Neither can the heirs or other parties in interest treat it as unqualifiedly void. They may confirm it either directly, or by their non-action continued for a long period of time, after having notice of the true nature of the transaction. Such, at least, is the opinion of the majority of the authorities.[1] In some of the cases, however, such a sale appears to have been held void.[2] In New York, it is made void by statute.[3] Sales made by sheriffs and constables, and in which they are interested, are, under the statutes in force in many of the States, held void.[4]

A sale to an administrator or guardian, where he is not the officer conducting the sale, as where it is made under an execution against his ward or intestate, while perhaps not so objectionable as a sale made in his official capacity, is, nevertheless, treated with no greater indulgence. The title

---

660; Miles v. Wheeler, 43 Ill. 123; Ives v. Ashley, 97 Mass. 198; Bailey v. Robinson, 1 Gratt. 4; s. c., 42 Am. Dec. 540; Edmunds v. Crenshaw, 1 McCord's Ch. 252; Glass v. Greathouse, 20 Oh. 503; Guerrero v. Ballerino, 48 Cal. 118; Scott v. Freeland, 7 S. & M. 409; s. c., 45 Am. Dec. 310; Green v. Sargeant, 23 Vt. 466; s. c., 56 Am. Dec. 88.

[1] Litchfield v. Cudworth, 15 Pick. 23; Munn v. Burges, 70 Ill. 604; Boyd v. Blankman, 29 Cal. 19; Hicks v. Weems, 14 La. An. 629; Musselman v. Eshelman, 10 Pa. St. 394; s. c., 51 Am. Dec. 493. See also the authorities in the preceding citation, and White v. Iselin, 26 Minn. 487; Fuller v. Little, 59 Ga. 338; Murphy v. Teter, 56 Ind. 545; Temples v. Cain, 60 Miss. 478; Davidson v. Davidson, 28 La. An. 269; Flanders v. Flanders, 23 Ga. 249; s. c., 68 Am. Dec. 523; Remick v. Butterfield, 31 N. H. 70; s. c., 64 Am. Dec. 316; Bland v. Muncaster, 24 Miss. 62; s. c., 57 Am. Dec. 162; Burch v. Lantz, 2 Rawle, 392; s. c., 21 Am. Dec. 458.

[2] Hamblin v. Warnecke, 31 Tex. 94; Morgan v. Wattles, 69 Ind. 260. Howell v. Tyler, 91 N. C. 207; Scott v. Gordon's Ex., 14 La. 115; s. c., 33 Am. Dec. 578.

[3] Terwilliger v. Brown, 44 N. Y. 237.

[4] Freeman on Executions, sec. 292; Woodbury v. Parker, 19 Vt. 353; s. c., 47 Am. Dec. 695; Chandler v. Moulton, 33 Vt. 247; Harrison v. McHenry, 9 Ga. 164; s. c., 52 Am. Dec. 435. Perhaps, by the concurrence, both of plaintiff and defendant, a constable's sale to himself may be ratified and become valid. Farnum v. Perry, 43 Vt. 473.

acquired thereat would doubtless be treated as held in trust for the benefit of the ward or heirs, and they could compel a conveyance to them on reimbursing the guardian or administrator for the money necessarily expended in the purchase.

In Arkansas, the attorney who prepares the petition for and obtains an order of sale, and the judge who grants such order, are incompetent to become purchasers at the sale.[1] We doubt the correctness of the decisions, holding that the attorney of a guardian or administrator is, by public policy, forbidden from becoming a purchaser at a sale made by such guardian or administrator.[2]

§ 34. **Sales to Raise too Great a Sum.**—In Kentucky, an execution or chancery sale to raise a sum greater than that authorized by the judgment or decree, is void.[3] A like rule seems to apply to probate sales in a few of the States.[4] How this rule can with any propriety be enforced against probate or chancery sales we are unable to imagine or understand. These sales take place under the authority of courts exercising jurisdiction over the owners of the property sold, and are reported to and confirmed by such courts, and when so confirmed the parties in interest then properly before the court are concluded by the order of confirmation. This is conceded in Kentucky, with respect to all sales reported to and confirmed by the court.[5] And we think that even in the case of execution sales, which the court is not required to confirm, that the sale of more property than was required to satisfy the judgment is a mere irregularity, for which the sale may be vacated; but

---

[1] West v. Waddell, 33 Ark. 575; Livingston v. Cochran, 33 Ark. 294.
[2] Grayson v. Weddle, 63 Mo. 523.
[3] Patterson v. Carneal, 3 A. K. Marsh. 618; s. c., 13 Am. Dec. 208; Blakely v. Abert, 1 Dana, 185; Hastings v. Johnson, 1 Nev. 613.
[4] Litchfield v. Cudworth, 15 Pick. 23; Lockwood v. Sturtevant, 6 Conn. 373; Adams v. Morrison, 4 N. H. 166; s. c., 17 Am. Dec. 406; Wakefield v. Campbell, 20 Me. 393; s. c., 37 Am. Dec. 60.
[5] Dawson v. Litsey, 10 Bush. 408.

that until vacated by some appropriate proceeding it is valid.[1]

§ 35. **Sales of Property Not Subject to Sale.**—It is always indispensable that the property sold should be subject to the license, decree or writ under which the sale is made. If an execution issues, it can reach the property of the defendant only. If the property of a stranger is seized and sold, his title is not divested thereby.[2] If property of the defendant is sold, it must be subject to the execution levied upon it, or the proceeding will be entirely inoperative upon his title.[3] Hence, an execution sale of a homestead is usually void;[4] and the same rule is often applied to other exempt property.[5] The property claimed as a homestead may be in excess of the quantity which the claimant is entitled to hold. In such cases, the statute generally provides some mode by which the non-exempt part may be severed from the exempt part and subjected to the satisfaction of the writ. A sale in the absence of such severance is void *in toto*.[6] If, under the statute of a State, the homestead of a decedent does not come within the control of its probate courts, an administrator's sale thereof, though ordered and confirmed by the court, is an idle proceeding.[7] If, while acting under a valid decree or license, an administrator sells lands not embraced therein,

---

[1] Groff v. Jones, 6 Wend. 522; Tiernan v. Wilson, 6 Johns. Ch. 411; Aldrich v. Wilcox, 10 R. I. 405; Osgood v. Blackmore, 59 Ill. 261; Weaver v. Guyer, 59 Ind. 195.

[2] Freeman on Executions, sec. 335.

[3] Ib., sec. 109.

[4] Ib., sec. 239.

[5] Ib., sec. 215.

[6] Owens v. Hart, 52 Ia. 620; s. c., 17 N. W. Rep. 898; Mebane v. Layton, 89 N. C. 396; Kipp v. Bullard, 30 Minn. 84; Mohan v. Smith, 30 Minn. 259.

[7] Yarboro v. Brewster, 38 Tex. 397; Hamblin v. Warnecke, 31 Tex. 93; Howe v. McGivern, 25 Wis. 525. This is true, though the sale is authorized to be made, and purports to be made subject to the homestead right. Wehrle v. Wehrle, 39 Oh. St. 365.

his act is, as to such lands, obviously without any legal support.[1]

§ 36. **Sales of a Different or Less Interest** than that of which the judgment debtor, or the estate of the decedent was seized, have, in several instances, been adjudged to be void. Thus, a sale which purported to be subject to a mortgage, when the mortgage had previously been fully satisfied, was adjudged to be wholly inoperative. "As to the tract which was levied on and sold, subject to the mortgage, we are of the opinion that nothing but the equity of redemption can be considered as having been sold; and that if the mortgage had previously been paid off, so that there was no subsisting mortgage and no equity of redemption, nothing passed by the sale and sheriff's deed."[2] So, an administrator's sale, under an order "to sell the equitable interest of the estate, when the decedent held a complete title, legal as well as equitable, was held to pass nothing to the purchaser;[3] and a like conclusion was reached when an undivided interest was ordered to be sold, when the decedent was seized of an estate in severalty.[4] Most of the decisions on this subject are not very clear in their statements of the reasons which were thought sufficient to justify their existence. The only substantial ground for their justification is that neither the officers charged with the seizure and sale of property, nor the courts invested with jurisdiction over the estates of minors or decedents, were intended to be given power to carve a complete and perfect title into distinct estates or interests, thereby making the subject-matter of the sale less inviting to purchasers, and, probably, leading to a needless sacrifice.

§ 37. **A Sale of an Undesignated** or unlocated part, as of a certain number of acres out of a larger parcel, when volun-

---

[1] Ludlow v. Park, 4 Oh. 5; Green v. Holt, 76 Mo. 677.
[2] Dougherty v. Linthicum, 8 Dana, 198; Bullard v. Hinkley, 6 Greenl. 289; s. c., 20 Am. Dec. 304.
[3] Crane v. Guthrie, 47 Ia. 542.
[4] Eberstein v. Oswalt, 47 Mich. 254.

tarily made, is sustained, and the grantee is allowed to locate his purchase and until such location is treated as a tenant in common with his grantor; but like indulgence is not conceded to the purchaser at an execution sale under like circumstances. On the contrary, his purchase is adjudged to be void for uncertainty.[1]

§ 38. **Sales of Property in Adverse Possession.**—The policy of the common law prohibited the transfer of causes of action. Lands of which the owner was disseized could not be conveyed during such disseizin. The conveyance of such lands was, by statute (32 Henry 8, c. 9), a crime for which, on conviction, both vendor and vendee were subject to the forfeiture of the value of the lands sought to be conveyed. Execution and judicial sales have never been within this inhibition against voluntary transfers. On the contrary, they are supported, whether he whose title is involuntarily transferred be seized or disseized.[2]

§ 39. **Sales en Masse.**—The duty of an officer in making a sale is to offer the property in such parcels as will prove most inviting to the bidders, and realize the greatest sums for the heirs and other interested persons. Hence, if several parcels of real estate be embraced in one license, the administrator is to offer them for sale, not in one lump, but "in such parcels as shall be best calculated to secure the greatest aggregate amount."[3] Where several distinct parcels of land are to be sold, each ought to be offered and sold separately, unless it is clear that the union of two or more will augment rather than decrease the aggregate proceeds of the sale. In Tennessee and Michigan, a lumping execution

---

[1] Pemberton v. McRae, 75 N. C. 497; Wooters v. Arledge, 54 Tex. 395; Freeman on Executions, sec. 281.

[2] Drinkwater v. Drinkwater, 4 Mass. 354; Willard v. Nason, 5 Mass. 241; High v. Nelms, 14 Ala. 350; s. c., 48 Am. Dec. 103; Cook v. Travis, 20 N. Y. 400; McGill v. Doe, 9 Ind. 306; Stevens v. Hauser, 39 N. Y. 302. *Contra*, Campbell v. P. S. I. Works, 12 R. I. 452.

[3] Delaplaine v. Lawrence, 3 N. Y. 304.

sale of two or more separate parcels of land is void;[1] but in nearly, if not quite all, the other States, such a sale, though voidable, is not a nullity.[2] In Michigan, a probate sale is not void, because two or more parcels are sold together.[3]

§ 40. **Sales Infected by Fraudulent Combinations and Devices.**—Judicial and execution sales are usually imperative. Those who own property are compelled to sell for whatever is offered. To avoid the sacrifice likely to ensue, notices of sale are required to be given, the property is struck off to the highest bidder, and competition among the persons intending to bid is sought to be produced. But the bidders, on their part, may enter into combinations and devices, either with one another or the officer conducting the sale, by means of which competition is lessened or altogether avoided. Every scheme looking to this result is highly immoral, and will, if possible, be thwarted by the courts. The sale may be vacated, either by motion or by a bill in equity. "Whether a purchase, obtained by the prevention of competition, can, by the guilty party, be asserted at law, is a question upon which the courts are by no means agreed. In several of the States such a purchase, and the deed made in pursuance thereof, are regarded as a valid transfer of the legal title. The defendant in execution, wishing to prevent the assertion of this title, must claim the assistance of a court of equity. But the majority of the decisions sustains an adverse theory—one under which

---

[1] Freeman on Executions, sec. 296; Mays v. Wherry, 58 Tenn. 133.

[2] Freeman on Executions, sec. 296; Bouldin v. Ewart, 63 Mo. 330; Foley v. Kane, 53 Ia. 64; Smith v. Schultz, 68 N. Y. 41; Lamberton v. Merchants' Bank, 24 Minn. 281; Rector v. Hartt, 8 Mo. 448; s. c., 41 Am. Dec. 650; Wilson v. Twitty, 14 Am. Dec. 569; s. c., 3 Hawks. 44. Indiana and Pennsylvania, though inclined to proceed with caution, will, doubtless, when necessity for further action arises, "fall into line" with the majority of their sister States. Jones v. Kokomo R. Association, 77 Ind. 340; Smith v. Meldren, 107 Pa. 348.

[3] Osman v. Traphagen, 23 Mich. 80.

the title of the fraudulent purchaser is, while in his hands, regarded as void, and, therefore, as capable of being resisted not less successfully at law than in equity."[1]

§ 41. **Purchaser's Title Not Affected by Secret Frauds.**—It is a general rule that one who purchases at a judicial, probate or execution sale cannot be deprived of his title by secret frauds or irregularities, in which he did not participate and of which he had no notice.[2] Hence, an administrator's sale cannot be avoided by showing that he procured his license to sell by fraud and misrepresentation in the absence of any necessity, and with the design of sacrificing the interests intrusted to his care.[3] Nor can an innocent purchaser be injuriously affected by proof of any mistake, error or fraud of an administrator or guardian in conducting a sale.[4] Although the original purchaser has himself been guilty of fraudulent devices, or has had notice of such devices practiced by others, he can transmit a valid, unimpeachable title to a vendee for value, in good faith, and without notice. Therefore, if a sale be nominally made to a stranger, but really for the benefit of the administrator, and this stranger convey to another, for value, who has no notice that the apparent are not the true facts, the title cannot, in the hands of the latter or his vendees, be rendered void or voidable by proof of the real facts.[5] The fact that the purchaser did not pay the amount of his bid

---

[1] Freeman on Executions, sec. 297; Underwood v. McVeigh, 23 Gratt. 409; Burton v. Spiers, 92 N. C. 503; Cram v. Rotherinel, 98 Pa. St. 300; Barton v. Hunter, 101 Pa. St. 406.

[2] Freeman on Executions, secs. 342, 353; Wisdom v. Parker, 31 La. An. 52; Herriman's Heirs v. Janney, 31 La. An. 276; Duckworth v. Vaughan, 27 La. An. 599; Zeigler v. Shomo, 78 Pa. St. 357; Maina v. Elliott, 51 Cal. 8; Wallace v. Loomis, 97 U. S. 146.

[3] Lamothe v. Lippott, 40 Mo. 142; Myer v. McDougal, 47 Ill. 278; Moore v. Neil, 39 Ill. 256; McCown v. Foster, 33 Tex. 211.

[4] Gwinn v. Williams, 30 Ind. 374; Staples v. Staples, 24 Gratt. 225; Jones v. Clark, 25 Gratt. 632; Patterson v. Lemon, 50 Ga. 231.

[5] Blood v. Hayman, 13 Met. 231; Staples v. Staples, 23 Gratt. 225; Robbins v. Bates, 4 Cush. 101; Gwinn v. Williams, 30 Ind. 374.

until several months after the sale, while it may, as between the purchaser and the defendant, entitle the latter to have the period allowed for redemption computed from the day of such payment rather than from the day of sale, cannot prejudice the title of an innocent purchaser who bought in good faith, relying upon the sheriff's deed.[1] A purchaser at a guardian's or administrator's sale is not charged with the duty of seeing to the proper application of the proceeds of the sale.[2] The validity of his title is not destroyed by the embezzlement of the money which he has paid to the person authorized by law to receive it.[3] The title of the purchaser at an execution sale is generally not dependent on the officer's return, and a failure to make such return does not avoid it,[4] neither is it imperiled by defects and variances in such return when made.[5]

---

[1] Maina v. Elliott, 51 Cal. 8; but there are cases holding that the fact of non-payment of the purchase money makes void a probate sale. Corbitt v. Clenny, 52 Ala. 480; Wallace v. Nichols, 56 Ala. 321.

[2] Cooper v. Horner, 62 Tex. 356; Knotts v. Stears, 91 U. S. 638; Barnes v. Trenton Gas L. Co., 27 N. J. Eq. 33; Whitman v. Fisher, 74 Ill. 147.

[3] Giles v. Pratt, 1 Hill (S. C.) 239; s. c., 26 Am. Dec. 170; Mulford v. Stalzenback, 46 Ill. 303; Muskingum Bank v. Carpenter, 7 Oh., part 1, p. 21.

[4] Bray v. Marshall, 75 Mo. 327; Holman v. Gill, 107 Ill. 467; Caldwell v. Blake, 69 Me. 458; Freeman on Executions, sec. 341. *Contra*, Walsh v. Anderson, 135 Mass. 65.

[5] Freeman on Executions, sec. 311; Hebbert v. Smith, 3 W. C. Rep. 446; Millis, v. Lombard, 32 Minn. 541; Ritter v. Scammell, 11 Cal. 238; s. c., 70 Am. Dec. 775.

CHAPTER IV.

THE CONFIRMATION AND DEED.

SECTION.
- 42. Notice must be Given before Confirming Sales.
- 43. Confirmation is Essential to Title.
- 44. What Irregularities are Cured by Confirmation.
- 45. Deed is Essential to Transfer of Legal Title.
- 46. Deed, When and by Whom, may be Made.
- 47. Deed when Void, because not in Proper Form.

§ 42. **Notice Before Confirmation.**—Under the statutes in force in most of the States, execution sales are not required to be approved by the court out of which the writ issued. Chancery and probate sales, on the other hand, are usually made subject to the approval of the court. In order to obtain this approval some of the statutes require a verified return of sales to be filed, and that this return shall be brought on for hearing only after notice has been given in a mode prescribed by statute. Where this is the case, the question arises whether a confirmation entered without giving any such notice is valid. The authorities on the subject are too meagre to justify any positive answer, but their tendency is toward the conclusion that the confirmation is a nullity, or, at least, that the confirmation does not preclude the parties from urging, in a collateral attack, any objections existing against the sale.[1]

[1] Speck v. Wohlien, 22 Mo. 310; Perkins v. Gridley, 50 Cal. 97; Dugger v. Tayloe, 60 Ala. 504; but in this State it is the administrator, and not the heirs, who must be notified.

§ 43. **Confirmation is Essential to Title.**—When the law under which a sale is made requires it to be reported to court for approval or disapproval, such approval is essential to the consummation of the sale. Without it there is no authority for making any conveyance to the purchaser,[1] and a conveyance without authority is obviously void.[2] This rule is equally applicable to execution, chancery and probate sales.[3] But instances may occur in which the ratification or acquiescence of the parties may either estop them from invoking this rule or give rise to the presumption that an order of confirmation was made, of which the evidence has been lost.[4] So, the approval of the court has sometimes been inferred from its subsequent acts and proceedings, though no order of confirmation could be found in its record.[5] The failure of the clerk of the court to enter the decree of confirmation on the minutes of the court is not fatal to the purchaser's title, where it sufficiently appears that such decree was in fact ordered by the court.[6]

§ 44. **What Irregularities are Cured by Confirmation.**—In Kansas, the confirmation by the court of an execution sale " is an adjudication merely that the proceedings

[1] McBain v. McBain, 15 Oh. St. 337; Curtis v. Norton, 1 Oh. 137.
[2] Williamson v. Berry, 8 How. (U. S.) 496; Gowan v. Jones, 10 S. & M. 164; Dickerson v. Talbot, 14 B. Mon. 60; Kable v. Mitchell, 9 W. Va. 492; Jones v. Hollingsworth, 10 Heisk. 653; Battell v. Toney, 65 N. Y. 299.
[3] Mason v. Osgood, 64 N. C. 467; Rawlins v. Bailey, 15 Ill. 178; Valle v. Fleming, 19 Mo. 454; Wallace v. Hall, 19 Ala. 367; Rea v. McEachron, 13 Wend. 465; s. c., 28 Am. Dec. 476; Bonner v. Greenlee, 6 Ala. 411; Wade v. Carpenter, 4 Ia. 361; State v. Towl, 48 Mo. 148.
[4] Henderson v. Herrod, 23 Miss. 434; Tipton v. Powell, 2 Coldw. 19; Smith v. West, 64 Ala. 34; Watts v. Scott, 3 Watts, 79; Gowan v. Jones, 10 S. & M. 164; Moore v. Greene, 19 How. (U. S.) 69. In some cases the confirmation of probate sales is not required by statute. Hobson v. Ewan, 62 Ill. 146; Robert v. Casey, 25 Mo. 584. In Missouri, the sale of lands under an order of the probate court must be confirmed; but confirmation is not indispensable to sales in proceedings before the circuit court. State v. Towl, 48 Mo. 148; Castleman v. Relfe, 50 Mo. 583.
[5] Grayson v. Weddle, 63 Mo. 523; Robertson v. Johnson, 57 Tex. 62.
[6] Koehler v. Ball, 2 Kans. 172.

of the officer, as they appear of record, are regular, and a direction to the sheriff to complete the sale."[1] With respect to chancery and probate sales, we apprehend that their confirmation has an effect beyond that conceded in Kansas to the confirmation of execution sales. The object of the proceeding for confirmation is to furnish an opportunity for inquiry respecting the acts which have been done under the license to sell. The court may, if it deems best, ratify various irregularities in the proceedings. If the officer changed the terms of the sale, the court may ratify his action, provided the terms, as changed, are such as the court had power to impose in the first instance.[2] As to the matters upon which a court is required to adjudicate in its order of confirmation, we see no reason why its decision should not be binding, and should not preclude the re-assertion of any matter which was either passed upon by the court, or which the parties might have had passed upon if they had chosen to bring it to the attention of the court.[3] After a sale has been confirmed, it cannot be defeated by showing collaterally that there was a failure to appraise the property,[4] or a defect in the notices of sale,[5] or that the administrator did not exact security for the payment of the purchase money,[6] or that the commissioner who made the sale, was not authorized to make it.[7] The code of civil procedure of California, declares, with respect to probate sales, that "all sales must be under oath, reported to and

---

[1] Moody v. Butler, 63 Tex. 210.
[2] Jacob's Appeal, 23 Pa. St. 477; Emery v. Vroman, 19 Wis. 689; Thorn v. Ingram, 25 Ark. 58.
[3] Willis v. Nicholson, 24 La. An. 545; Cockey v. Cole, 28 Md. 276; Hotchkiss v. Cutting, 14 Minn. 537; Brown v. Gilmor, 8 Md. 322; Thorn v. Ingram, 25 Ark. 58; Osman v. Traphagen, 23 Mich. 80; Conover v. Musgrove, 68 Ill. 58; McRae v. Danner, 8 Org. 63; Dawson v. Litsey, 10 Bush. 408.
[4] Neligh v. Keene, 16 Neb. 407; s. c., 20 N. W. Rep. 277.
[5] Wyant v. Tuthill, 17 Neb. 495; s. c., 23 N. W. Rep. 342.
[6] Wilkerson v. Allen, 67 Mo. 502.
[7] Core v. Stricker, 24 W. Va. 689.

confirmed by the court, before the title to the property sold passes." In an action of ejectment, it appeared that defendant's title was based on a probate sale; that the return of sales, as offered and received in evidence, was not verified, but that the order of confirmation contained a recital, "that the return of sale was duly verified by affidavit." The court said: "This recital is conclusive in the present case, and a finding of fact to the contrary does not in any manner affect the conclusiveness of the recital in the decree. The fact was not a jurisdictional one, and the principle applicable to the inconclusiveness of statements, or recitals in judgments, conferring jurisdiction, does not apply."[1] But the curative powers of orders of confirmation extend to voidable, rather than to void. If a sale be void because the court did not have jurisdiction to order it, an order confirming it is necessarily inoperative. "The sale being void, there was no subject-matter upon which the order of confirmation could act. If the court had no jurisdiction to order the sale, it had none to confirm it. Where there is no power to render a judgment, or to make an order, there can be none to confirm or execute it."[2] If, after property is sold at probate sale to the highest bidder, he fails to comply with his bid, and another person is substituted in his place, and is reported to the court as the purchaser, and the sale is confirmed to the latter, he cannot avoid the sale and be exonerated from paying the purchase price. "The mere substitution of one person for another cannot affect the validity of the sale. The order directing the sale, and the order confirming it, give vitality the purchase."[3]

---

[1] Dennis v. Winter, 63 Cal. 16.
[2] Minn. Co. v. St. Paul Co., 2 Wall. 609; Pike v. Wassall, 94 U. S. 74. Townsend v. Tallant, 33 Cal. 54; Shriver v. Lynn, 2 How. (U. S.) 57; Hawkins v. Hawkins, 28 Ind. 70. See Bethel v. Bethel, 6 Bush. 65.
[3] Halleck v. Guy, 9 Cal. 197; s. c., 70 Am. Dec. 643; Ewing v. Higby, 7 Oh., pt. p. 198.

§ 45. **Deed Essential to the Transfer of Legal Title.**—A conveyance is necessary to invest the purchaser, at an execution, chancery or probate sale, with the legal title.[1] In Maryland and Texas, this rule seems not to apply to execution sales,[2] though in the last named State, a conveyance by an administrator is conceded to be essential to the transfer of the legal title after a probate sale.[3]

§ 46. **Deed, When and by Whom to be Made.**—In Massachusetts and Maine, under statutes prescribing that licenses for sales should continue in force for one year only after they were given, it was held that the execution of a deed was a part of the sale, and that, if not executed within one year after the granting of the license, it was void.[4] We cannot concur in this opinion. A sale is certainly complete when it has been regularly confirmed by the court, and the purchase price has been paid to the person entitled to receive it. Even if this be not true, the purchaser has acquired an equitable title—a right to a conveyance in pursuance of his purchase and payment. A court of equity would recognize and protect this right, by decreeing a conveyance.[5] If a conveyance can be compelled, certainly it ought not to be void merely because made without compulsion.[6] No conveyance ought to be made before the payment of the purchase money.[7] If made before such payment, it is void in Indiana.[8] But, we apprehend that,

[1] Freeman on Executions, sec. 324; Merrit v. Terry, 13 Johns. 471; Doe v. Hardy, 52 Ala. 291; Hudgens v. Jackson, 51 Ala. 514; Van Alstyne v. Wimple, 5 Cow. 162; Farmers' Bank v. Merchant, 13 How. Pr. 10.

[2] Boring v. Lemmon, 5 H. & J. 223; Leland v. Wilson, 34 Tex. 91; Fleming v. Powell, 2 Tex. 225.

[3] Sypert v. McCowen, 28 Tex. 638.

[4] Macy v. Raymond, 9 Pick. 287; Wellman v. Lawrence, 15 Mass. 326; Mason v. Ham, 36 Me. 573.

[5] Piatt's Heirs v. McCullough's Heirs, 1 McLean, 69.

[6] Howard v. Moore, 2 Mich. 226; Osman v. Traphagen, 23 Mich. 80.

[7] Barnes v. Morris, 4 Ired. Eq. 22.

[8] Ruckle v. Barbour, 48 Ind. 274; Chapman v. Harwood, 8 Blackf. 82. In Alabama, an order to convey before all the purchase money is paid, is a nullity. Corbitt v. Clenny, 52 Ala. 480.

as a general rule, such a conveyance is voidable rather than
void.¹ If the statute, under which a sale is made, does not
authorize a conveyance until after the expiration of the
time allowed the defendant to redeem his property, a deed
made in advance of that time is a nullity.² After the right
to a deed has become perfect, we believe it may be made at
any time. An administrator's, executor's or guardian's
deed must be made in person. These officers exercise
powers in the nature of trusts, wherein special confidence is
reposed. Hence, they cannot delegate their authority to
agents.³ Sheriffs and constables, on the other hand, may
have deputies, and such deputies are competent to execute
conveyances in the names of their principals.⁴ In Mississippi, an administrator *de bonis non* cannot execute a conveyance where the sale was made by his predecessor in
office.⁵ But we judge the better rule to be, that such an
administrator may complete whatever the first administrator
ought to have done.⁶ A conveyance made to a person not
entitled to receive it, as where a deed is given to one as
assignee, when no assignment has been made, is void.⁷

§ 47. **Deed, when Void because not in Proper Form.**—
The instances in which a deed, issued in pursuance of an
execution or chancery sale, is void for errors, defects or
mistakes in form, are very rare. In fact, any instrument
executed by an officer authorized to make it, purporting to
convey the property, is probably sufficient, if the acts necessary to authorize him to make a conveyance can be shown.⁸
Of course, the deed must be executed with the formalities
essential to other deeds, and must show that the person

---

[1] Osman v. Traphagen, 23 Mich. 80.
[2] Freeman on Executions, sec. 316.
[3] Gridley v. Phillips, 5 Kans. 349.
[4] Freeman on Executions, sec. 327.
[5] Davis v. Brandon, 1 How. (Miss.) 154.
[6] Gridley v. Phillips, 5 Kans. 354.
[7] Carpenter v. Sherfy, 71 Ill. 427.
[8] Freeman on Executions, sec. 329.

§ 47 VOID JUDICIAL SALES.

who signs it, is acting in an official capacity, and not merely conveying his own title to the property. In some States a form for sheriff's deeds is prescribed by statute. These statutes are generally, but not universally, declared to be directory merely.[1] Deeds executed by executors, administrators or guardians, are, in many States, treated with less indulgence than those made by sheriffs. This is particularly the case where a statute has directed that some statement or recital shall be set forth in a deed. Such statutes, with reference to administrator's and guardian's deeds, have been held imperative, and not directory merely. Thus, where a statute required an order to be set forth at large, a deed merely referring to such order, and stating its substance, was adjudged void.[2] The correctness of this decision may be doubted; but it is certain that an omission to refer to an order, or a reference which did not fully describe the order, would, under a statute similar to the one just alluded to, render the deed void.[3] Although a statute requires the order of sale, and also that of confirmation, to be referred to or set out in the deed, a mere mistake in the reference is not fatal, if it appears from the deed, taken as a whole, that the reference, as made, is a mistake, and that it was intended to embrace the orders under which the sale and deed were, in fact, made.[4] The same rule applies to mistakes and omissions in the recitals in deeds, made in pursuance of execution sales.[5] Irrespective of any statu-

---

[1] Freeman on Executions, sec. 329; Armstrong v. McCoy, 8 Oh. 128; s. c., 31 Am. Dec. 435; Bettison v. Budd, 17 Ark. 558; Ogden v. Walters, 12 Kans. 290; Perkins' Lessee v. Dibble, 10 Oh. 433; s. c., 36 Am. Dec. 97; Holman v. Gill, 107 Ill. 467.

[2] Smith v. Finch, 1 Scam. 323.

[3] Atkins v. Kinnan, 20 Wend. 241; s. c., 32 Am. Dec. 534.

[4] Sheldon v. Wright, 5 N. Y. 497; Thomas v. Le Baron, 8 Met. 361; Jones v. Taylor, 7 Tex. 242; Moore v. Wingate, 53 Mo. 398; Glover v. Ruflin, 6 Oh. 255; Clark v. Sawyer, 48 Cal. 133; Mitchell v. Bliss, 47 Mo. 353; Speck v. Riggins, 40 Mo. 405; Davis v. Kline, 76 Mo. 310; Williams v. Woodman, 73 Me. 163.

[5] Freeman on Executions, sec. 329; Brooks v. Rooney, 11 Ga. 423; s. c., 56 Am. Dec. 430; Gourdin v. Davis, 45 Am. Dec. 745; Howard v.

tory directions on the subject, every administrator's, executor's or guardian's deed should refer to the authority or license under which it is made; should state that the person making it acted under such license; and should contain apt words to convey the estate of the ward or decedent, as contradistinguished from the private estate of the person executing the deed;[1] but it need not recite all the steps taken in making the sale, as that the sale was at public auction, and that the grantee was the highest bidder.[2] Where statutes exist, directing what recitals shall be set forth in sheriff's deeds, occasional decisions may be found declaring such deeds void, because of their non-compliance with the statute. These decisions will generally be found restricted to cases where the omission in the deed was of a matter absolutely essential to the support of the sale, as the omission to recite the judgment,[3] or the time of the sale, where sales can, under the statute, take place only at certain designated times, for instance, during the term of the court.[4] In other words, the deed must show an authority to sell, and that such authority was pursued substantially as prescribed by law. Beyond this, even in the States where statutes undertake to specify the recitals to be inserted in a sheriff's deed, omissions and misrecitals are not fatal.[5]

North, 51 Am. Dec. 769; Haskins v. Wallet, 63 Tex. 213; Phillips v. Coffee, 17 Ill. 154; s. c., 63 Am. Dec. 357; Keith v. Keith, 104 Ill. 401; Humphrey v. Beeson, 1 G. Greene, 199; s. c., 48 Am. Dec. 370; Harrison v. Maxwell, 2 N. & M. C. 347; s. c., 10 Am. Dec. 611; McGuire v. Kouns, 7 Mon. 386; s. c., 18 Am. Dec. 187; Martin v. Wilbourne, 2 Hill, 395; s. c., 27 Am. Dec. 393; Hind's Heirs v. Scott, 11 Pa. St. 19; s. c., 51 Am. Dec. 506.

[1] Jones v. Taylor, 7 Tex. 242; Bobb v. Barnum, 59 Mo. 394; Griswold v. Bigelow, 6 Conn. 258; Lockwood v. Sturdevant, 6 Conn. 373. The two cases last named are limited in Watson v. Watson, 10 Conn. 77.

[2] Kingsbury v. Wild, 3 N. H. 30.

[3] Dufour v. Camfranc, 11 Mart. 607; s. c., 13 Am. Dec. 360.

[4] Tanner v. Stine, 18 Mo. 580; s. c., 59 Am. Dec. 320; Martin v. Bonsach, 61 Mo. 556.

[5] Buchanan v. Tracy, 45 Mo. 437; Strain v. Murphy, 49 Ind. 337.

CHAPTER V.

THE LEGAL AND EQUITABLE RIGHTS OF PURCHASERS AT VOID SALES.

SECTION.
48. Purchaser's Right to Resist the Payment of His Bid.
49. Purchaser's Right to Recover Money Paid.
50. Purchaser's Right to Urge Acts of Ratification as Estoppels in His Favor.
51. Purchaser's Right to Subrogation Denied.
52. Purchaser's Right to Subrogation Affirmed, under Execution and Chancery Sales.
53. Purchaser's Right to Subrogation Affirmed, under Probate Sales.
54. Purchaser's Right to Subrogation, where he is Guilty of Fraud.
55. Purchaser's Right to Aid of Equity in Supplying Omissions and Correcting Mistakes.

§ 48. **Purchaser's Right to Resist the Payment of His Bid.**—If the purchaser at a void execution or judicial sale, be so fortunate as to discover the true character and effect of the sale, prior to the actual payment of the purchase price, he will, of course, seek to avoid making such payment. No doubt the bidder at a void sale is entitled to be released from his bid. "The purchaser at a partition sale is entitled to the whole title partitioned. If, from any irregularities or defects in the suit or in the proceedings, the purchaser would not, by completing his bid and receiving his conveyance, become invested with the whole title with which the court assumed to deal, then he will be released from his bid. Hence, if jurisdiction has not been acquired over one of the co-tenants, the purchaser will be released."[1] So, in purchases under execution sales, the purchaser cannot be compelled to make payment, if the proceedings are so defective, in any respect, that they cannot divest the title of the judgment debtor.[2] Every purchaser has a right to suppose that, by his purchase, he will obtain the title of the defendant in execution, in case of execution sales, and of the ward or decedent in the case of a guardian's or administrator's sale. The promise to convey this title, is the consideration upon which his bid is made. If the judgment or order of sale is void, or if, from any cause, the conveyance, when made, cannot invest him with the title held by the parties to the suit or proceeding, then his bid, or other promise to pay, is without consideration, and cannot be enforced. He may successfully resist any action for the purchase money, whether based upon the bid or upon some bond or note given by him.[3] In Mississippi, however, he cannot avoid paying the purchase price of personal property of which he has obtained, and still retains possession by virtue of the sale.[4] The distinction between void sales and defective titles must be kept in view, to avoid any misapprehension of the rights of one who has purchased at an execution or judicial sale, without, in fact, obtaining anything. If he obtains nothing because of a defect in the proceedings, he can defeat an action for the amount of his bid. If, on the other hand, the proceedings are perfect,

---

[1] Freeman on Cotenancy and Partition, sec. 547.

[2] Freeman on Executions, sec. 301.

[3] Laughman v. Thompson, 6 S. & M. 259; Campbell v. Brown, 6 How. (Miss.) 230; Bartee v. Thompkins, 4 Sneed, 623; Todd v. Dowd, 1 Met. (Ky.) 281; Barrett v. Churchill, 18 B. Mon. 387; Washington v. McCaughan, 34 Miss. 304; Riddle v. Hill, 51 Ala. 224; Verdin v. Slocum, 71 N. Y. 345; Goode v. Crow, 51 Mo. 212; Boykin v. Cook, 61 Ala. 472; Burns v. Ledbetter, 56 Tex. 282; Dodd v. Neilson, 90 N. Y. 243; Threft v. Fritz, 7 Ill. App. 55; Short v. Porter, 44 Miss. 533; note to Burns v. Hamilton, 70 Am. Dec. 580.

[4] Washington v. McCaughan, 34 Miss. 304; Martin v. Tarver, 43 Miss. 517; Jaggers v. Griffin, 43 Miss. 134.

but the defendant, or ward, or decedent, had no title to be sold nor conveyed, the purchaser is nevertheless bound by his bid. *Caveat emptor* is the rule of all execution and judicial sales. Each bid is made for such title as the defendant, ward or decedent may have, and is, therefore, binding, whether either had title or not.[1] "But the better rule is that, in equity sales, the purchaser is entitled to receive a title free from equities and incumbrances of which he had no notice; and if, by the sale, he will not receive such title, he will not, on his making objection, be compelled to complete his purchase, but will be released therefrom, unless the title can be made good, or other just relief awarded."[2] The time for making objection is when the sale is reported for confirmation. The confirmation is binding on the purchaser, and after that he is precluded from objecting that the title was imperfect or incumbered, and thus avoiding the payment of his bid.[3]

[1] Freeman on Executions, sec. 301; Freeman on Cotenancy and Partition, sec. 517; Osterberg v. Union Trust Co., 93 U. S. 424; McManus v. Keith, 49 Ill. 389; Short v. Porter, 44 Miss. 533; Bassett v. Lockard, 60 Ill. 164; Boykin v. Cook, 61 Ala. 472; England v. Clark, 4 Scam. 486; Boro v. Harris, 13 Lea. 36; Holmes v. Shafer, 78 Ill. 578; Dunn v. Frazier, 8 Blackf. 432; Rodgers v. Smith, 2 Ind. 526: Dean v. Morris, 4 G. Greene, 312; Islay v. Stewart, 4 D. & B. 160; Richardson v. Vicker, 74 N. C. 278; Rollins v. Henry, 78 N. C. 342. The rule was applied against purchasers at probate sales in Worthington v. McRoberts, 9 Ala. 297; Jennings v. Jennings' Admr., Id., 291; Owen v. Slatter, 26 Ala. 547; s. c., 62 Am. Dec. 745; Byrd v. Turpin, 62 Ga. 591; Colbert v. Moore, 64 Id. 502; Tilley v. Bridges, 105 Ill. 336; London v. Robertson, 5 Blackf. 276; Cogan v. Frisby, 36 Miss. 185; Thompson v. Munger, 15 Tex. 523; s. c., 65 Am. Dec. 176; Burns v. Hamilton, 33 Ala. 210; s. c., 70 Am. Dec. 570; Jones v. Warnock, 67 Ga. 484; King v. Gunnison, 4 Pa. St. 171.

[2] Note to Burns v. Hamilton, 70 Am. Dec. 575, citing Scott v. Bentel, 23 Gratt. 1; Bolivar v. Zeigler, 9 S. C. 287; Monaghan v. Small, 6 S. C. 177; Kostenbader v. Spotts, 80 Pa. St. 430; Edney v. Edney, 80 N. C. 81; Monarque v. Monarque, 80 N. Y. 320; Hunting v. Walter 33 Md. 60.

[3] Osterberg v. Union Trust Co., 93 U. S. 424; Dresbach v. Stein, 41 Oh. St. 70; Mechanics' S. & B. Assn. v. O'Conner, 29 Oh. St. 651; Barron v. Mullin, 21 Minn. 374; Holmes v. Shaver, 78 Ill. 578; Thomas v. David-

§ 49. **The Purchaser's Right to Recover Back Money Paid.**—Whoever pays out money on account of a purchase made at a void sale, parts with a valuable consideration, for which he acquires nothing. The question then arising, is: Has the purchaser any remedy? and, if so, what is the remedy, and to what cases may it be applied with success? Where the plaintiff is the purchaser, he may, in most States, upon failure of his title, in effect vacate the apparent satisfaction produced by the sale, and obtain a new execution.[1] If the title fails through defects in the proceedings, arising from the neglect or misconduct of the sheriff, the purchaser can sustain an action on the case against that officer.[2] Where a purchase is made under a decree in equity, and such decree is reversed for a jurisdictional defect in the proceedings, or where the title fails because the grantee of a mortgagor was not a party to a foreclosure, the plaintiff has the right to prosecute further proceedings. In the case first named, he may have the process properly served, and thus give the court jurisdiction to proceed. In the second named case, he may apply to the court, have the sale vacated, the satisfaction cancelled, and then, by supplemental bill, bring in the proper parties, and have the property re-sold. In either case the purchaser may, by applying to the court in the original suit, have the proceedings conducted for his benefit, though in the name of the original plaintiff.[3] In New York and Tennessee, if the proceed-

---

son, 76 Va. 344; Hickson v. Rucker, 77 Va. 135; Long v. Weller, 29 Gratt. 347; Threlkelds v. Campbell, 2 Gratt. 198; s. c., 44 Am. Dec. 384; Capehart v. Dowery, 10 W. Va. 130; Farmers' Bank v. Peters, 13 Bush. 591; Housley v. Lindsey, 10 Heisk. 651; Anderson v. Foulks, 2 H. & G. 346; Farmers' Bank v. Martin, 7 Md. 342; s. c., 61 Am. Dec. 350; Bassett v. Lockard, 60 Ill. 164; Cashion v. Fania, 47 Mo. 133.

[1] Freeman on Executions, sec. 54; Sargent v. Sturm, 23 Cal. 359; Piper v. Elwood, 4 Den. 165; Adams v. Smith, 5 Cow. 280; Watson v. Reissig, 24 Ill. 281.

[2] Sexton v. Nevers, 20 Pick. 451.

[3] Boggs v. Hargrave, 16 Cal. 559; Burton v. Lies, 21 Cal. 87; Johnson v. Robertson, 34 Md. 165; Cook v. Toombs, 36 Miss. 685; Hudgin v.

ings are utterly void, the purchaser may recover from the plaintiff the amount paid upon the latter's judgment.[1] In Texas, if a sale under a valid judgment be void for defects in the proceedings, the purchaser is entitled to the property, unless the defendant will reimburse him for the amount he has paid toward satisfying the judgment.[2] In Kentucky, Indiana, Illinois and Texas, if the defendant in execution has no title, he may be compelled, by proceedings in equity, to reimburse the purchaser for the amount contributed by means of the purchase, to the satisfaction of the judgment.[3] But we think the better rule is that, unless proceeding upon the ground of fraud or misrepresentation, or some other well known ground, a purchaser at an execution sale cannot, by any independent action, recover of either of the parties the amount of his bid.[4] Such an action is, neces-

Hudgin, 6 Gratt. 320; s. c., 52 Am. Dec. 124. See, also, Scott v. Dunn, 1 D. & B. Eq. 425.

[1] Chapman v. Brooklyn, 40 N. Y. 372; Schwinger v. Hickok, 53 N. Y. 280; Henderson v. Overton, 2 Yerg. 394; s. c., 24 Am. Dec. 492. The principle upon which these cases profess to proceed is, that a party may recover moneys paid where there is a total failure of consideration. This principle is sufficiently supported by the authorities (Moses v. McFarlane, 2 Burr. 1009; Rheel v. Hices, 25 N. Y. 289; Kingston Bank v. Eltinge, 40 N. Y. 391;) but we doubt its applicability to execution sales.

[2] Johnson v. Caldwell, 38 Tex. 218; Howard v. North, 5 Tex. 290; s. c., 51 Am. Dec. 789. A person seeking to cancel a sheriff's deed as a cloud upon his title, must, in Texas, first repay the amount for which the property was sold by the sheriff. Herndon v. Rice, 21 Tex. 457; Morton v. Welborn, 21. Tex. 773; Brown v. Lane, 19 Tex. 205.

[3] McGhee v. Ellis, 4 Litt. 245; s. c., 16 Am. Dec. 124; Muir v. Craig, 3 Blackf. 293; s. c., 25 Am. Dec. 111; Warner v. Helm, 1 Gilm. 220; Price v. Boyd, 1 Dana, 436; Hawkins v. Miller, 26 Ind. 173; Preston v. Harrison, 9 Ind. 1; Jones v. Henry, 3 Litt. 435; Dunn v. Frazier, 8 Blackf. 432; Pennington v. Clifton, 10 Ind. 172; Richmond v. Marston, 15 Ind. 134; Julian v. Beal, 26 Ind. 220; Howard v. North, 5 Tex. 290; s. c., 51 Am. Dec. 769; Arnold v. Cord, 16 Ind. 177; Taylor v. Conner, 7 Ind. 115.

[4] Branham v. San Jose, 24 Cal. 585; Boggs v. Hargrave, 16 Cal. 559; Salmond v. Price, 13 Oh. 368; s. c., 42 Am. Dec. 204; Laws v. Thompson, 4 Jones, 104; Halcombe v. Loudermilk, 3 Jones, 491; The Monte Allegre, 9 Wheat. 616; Burns v. Hamilton, 33 Ala. 210.

sarily, founded upon a mistake of law. The purchaser is sure to base his claim upon the fact that he mistook the legal effect of the proceedings in the case, or of the defendant's muniments of title. And it is well known that a mistake of law is not a sufficient foundation for relief at law or in equity. The rule of *caveat emptor* unquestionably applies to judicial sales; and we know not how this rule can co-exist with another rule requiring one of the parties to indemnify the purchaser in the event of a failure of the title. In a few of the States, purchasers have been given a statutory remedy.[1] The purchaser at a void execution sale may, by the payment of his bid, wholly or partly discharge some lien or claim on the property purchased. The question then arising is this: Has he the right to hold the property until the amount thus paid is refunded to him? The consideration of this question is reserved for a subsequent section.[2]

§ 50. **Ratification of Void Sales by the Acts of the Parties in Interest.**—As a general rule, a confirmation or ratification cannot strengthen a void estate. "For confirmation may make a voidable or defeasible estate good, but cannot operate on an estate void in law."[3] If this rule be one of universal application, then there can be no necessity for considering the question of ratification in connection with void judicial sales. But this is one of those rules which are so limited by exceptions, that the circumstances to which it may be applied are scarcely more numerous than those from which its application must be withheld. There can now be scarcely any doubt that void judicial sales are within the exceptions, and are unaffected by the rule.[4]

---

[1] C. C. P. of Cal., sec. 708; Halcombe v. Loudermilk, 3 Jones, 491; Chambers v. Cochran, 18 Ia. 160.

[2] See secs. 51-53.

[3] Bouvier's Law Dic., title "Confirmation."

[4] Maple v. Kussart, 53 Pa. St. 348; Johnson v. Fritz, 44 Pa. St. 449; Deford v. Mercer, 24 Ia. 118; Pursley v. Hays, 17 Ia. 310; Johnson v. Cooper, 56 Miss. 608.

These sales may be ratified either directly or by a course of conduct which estops the party from denying their validity. Thus, if the defendant in execution, after a void sale of his property has been made, claims and receives the surplus proceeds of the sale, with a full knowledge of his rights, his act must thereafter be treated as an irrevocable confirmation of the sale.[1] In a case decided in Pennsylvania, a judgment was recovered against the administrator of an estate. The heirs of the decedent were not parties to the action in which this judgment were recovered, and were, therefore, under the laws of that State, unaffected by it. Under this judgment, writs were issued, and lands of the decedents levied upon, condemned and sold. They produced funds more than sufficient to satisfy the judgment. The surplus was paid to the heirs. One of the daughters having brought ejectment for the lands, the supreme court, in discussing and determining her rights, said: " She was perfectly acquainted with the *fact* that she had not been served with process to make her a party to the judgment on which the sale was made, and that she had not voluntarily made herself a party to that proceeding without process; and there is no evidence to repel the presumption that she was equally well acquainted with the rules of *law* which entitled her to disregard a sale made under such a judgment, as having no operation whatever upon her rights, unless she did some act which, on principles of equity and common honesty, might estop her from impeaching it. As she was not a defendant in the execution, she had no right, in that character, to receive any part of the money, after payment of the creditor's claim. Her only title to the money depended upon the effect of the proceedings in divesting her estate in the land, and converting it into money,

---

[1] Stroble v. Smith, 8 Watts, 280; Headen v. Oubre, 2 La. An. 142; Sittig v. Morgan, 5 La. An. 574; McLeod v. Johnson, 28 Miss. 374; Southard v. Perry, 21 Ia. 488; State v. Stanley, 14 Ind. 409; Crowell v. McConkey, 5 Pa. St. 168.

by passing her title to the purchasers. Upon this ground alone could she make any claim to the money, in law or equity. The receipt of her share of the money was, therefore, an affirmation that her title had passed to the purchasers by virtue of the sheriff's sale; and she cannot be received to make a contrary allegation now, to the injury of those who paid their money on the faith of the conveyance. Where a sale is made of land, no one can be permitted to receive both the money and the land. Even if the vendor possessed no title whatever at the time of the sale, the estoppel would operate upon a title subsequently acquired." It was held by this court, at the late sitting in Harrisburg, that " equitable estoppels of this character apply to infants as well as adults, to insolvent trustees and guardians as well as persons acting for themselves, and have place as well, where the proceeds arise from a sale *by authority of law*, as where they spring from *the act of the party*.[1] The application of this principle does not depend upon any supposed distinction between a void and voidable sale. The receipt of the money, with the knowledge that the purchaser is paying it upon an understanding that he is purchasing a good title, touches the conscience, and, therefore, binds the right of the party in one case as well as the other."[2] Perhaps it is not essential that the defendant in execution should have directly received any part of the proceeds of the sale. If he knows of the sale, makes no objections thereto, and permits the proceeds to be applied to the

---

[1] Commonwealth v. Shuman's Admr., 6 Harris, 346; McPherson v. Cunliff, 11 S. & R. 426; s. c., 14 Am. Dec. 642; Wilson v. Bigger, 7 W. & Ser. 111; Stroble v. Smith, 8 Watts, 280; Benedict v. Montgomery, 7 W. & Ser. 238; s. c., 43 Am. Dec. 230; Martin v. Ives, 17 Ser. & R. 364; Crowell v. McConkey, 5 Barr, 168; Hamilton v. Hamilton, 4 Barr, 193; Dean v. Connelly, 6 Barr, 239; Robinson v. Justice, 2 Pa. Rep. 19; Share v. Anderson, 7 Ser. & R. 48; s. c., 10 Am. Dec. 421; Furness v. Ewing, 2 Barr, 479; Adlum v. Yard, 1 Rawle, 163; s. c., 18 Am. Dec. 608.

[2] Smith v. Warden, 19 Pa. St. 429.

payment of his debts, he will, at least in Pennsylvania, be precluded from denying its validity.[1] If lands be sold at a partition or other chancery sale, no co-tenant, who has claimed and received his share of the proceeds, can deny the validity of the partition. He cannot be allowed to retain the money and regain the land.[2] The same principle applies to sales made by guardians, administrators and executors. A ward or heir may elect to affirm a void sale, and thus entitle himself to the proceeds.[3] When a valid election is once made, it cannot be revoked. The ratification by a ward or heir of a sale, made by an administrator or guardian, may be made also by receiving the proceeds of the sale.[4] Of course, this ratification cannot be accomplished through the action of a minor, or of any person not competent to act for himself.[5] If the person whose property was sold be a minor, he cannot ratify the sale until after he becomes of lawful age. Nor can anyone ratify for him during his minority. No act done or sanctioned by his guardian can bind him as a ratification; nor will he be held to affirm the sale merely on the ground that, during his minority, the proceeds were applied to his use or for his benefit,[6] nor because such proceeds were accounted for by the administrator in his settlements with the estate, no part being paid over to the heir.[7] In Missouri and Wisconsin,

[1] Spragg v. Shriver, 25 Pa. St. 282; s. c., 64 Am. Dec. 698; Mitchell v. Freedley, 10 Pa. St. 208; Maple v. Kussart, 53 Pa. St. 352; Williard v. Williard, 56 Pa. St. 128.

[2] Tooley v. Gridley, 3 S. & M. 493; s. c., 51 Am. Dec. 628; Merritt v. Horne, 5 Oh. St. 307; s. c., 67 Am. Dec. 298.

[3] Jennings v. Kee, 5 Ind. 257.

[4] Ib.; Lee v. Gardner, 26 Miss. 521; Pursley v. Hays, 17 Ia. 310; Deford v. Mercer, 24 Ia. 118; Wilson v. Bigger, 7 W. & S. 111; Handy v. Noonan, 51 Miss. 166; Parmelee v. McGinty, 52 Miss. 475; Walker v. Mulvean, 76 Ill. 18; Corwin v. Shoup, 76 Ill. 246.

[5] A *feme covert* may affirm a void sale by receiving the proceeds, Kempe v. Pintard, 32 Miss. 324.

[6] Requa v. Holmes, 26 N. Y. 338; Wilkinson v. Filby, 24 Wis. 441; Longworth v. Goforth, Wright, 192.

[7] Townsend v. Tallent, 33 Cal. 45.

the receipt of the proceeds of a guardian's sale by a minor after coming of age, or by a lunatic after becoming sane, does not operate as an affirmance of the sale.[1] The hardship of this rule is very materially ameliorated, in the States named, by the adoption of another rule, under which a *bona fide* purchaser of lands sold at a void judicial sale is entitled to retain, in many cases, a charge or lien on the property, for the amount paid by him. It is essential to every valid ratification, that the ratifying acts were done with a full knowledge of the facts constituting the transaction to be ratified.[2]

§ 51. **Right of Purchasers to be Subrogated to the Lien Discharged, Denied.**—A judicial or execution sale is usually made for the purpose of satisfying some lien or charge on the property sold. After such sale is made, and the amount of the bid paid, the owner of the property, if he can avoid the sale, will not only retain the property which was originally his, but will also have its value enhanced by the amount paid to remove the charge or lien therefrom. According to natural equity, it is clear that the owner ought not to thus to profit by the sale, and that the purchaser ought to be subrogated to the rights of the holder of the charge or lien. There is some doubt whether the equity which is, in fact, administered by the courts, enforces, in this case, what we deem to be the dictates of natural equity. In a case decided in Indiana, an execution sale was made under a valid judgment, but the sale itself was inoperative, on account of a non-compliance with the appraisement law. The purchaser, however, claimed that he was entitled in equity to be subrogated to the rights of the judgment creditor. The supreme court, in denying the claim, said: " Can the doctrine of subrogation be applied to the case made by the record? This is the main inquiry

---

[1] Valle v. Fleming, 19 Mo. 454; s. c., 61 Am. Dec. 566; Mohr v. Tulip, 40 Wis. 66.
[2] Dolargue v. Cress, 71 Ill. 380.

in the case. We are not advised of any direct adjudication on the point involved in this question; but there are various authorities to the effect that 'it is only in cases where the person paying the debt stands in the situation of a surety, or is compelled to pay in order to protect his own interest, or in virtue of legal process, that equity substitutes him in place of the creditor, as a matter of course, without any special agreement. A stranger paying the debt of another, will not be subrogated to the creditor's right, in the absence of an agreement to that effect; payment by such person absolutely extinguishes the debt and security.'[1] This exposition being correct, and we think it is, we are unable to perceive any ground upon which the decree, so far as it subrogates the plaintiffs to the rights of the judgment creditor, can be maintained. The position of Marston was that of an ordinary vendee at a sheriff's sale, and nothing more. There is, indeed, nothing in the case in any degree tending to show that the protection of his interest required, or even induced, the purchase. He purchased the land and paid for it voluntarily; we must, therefore, hold that the amount which he paid to the sheriff operated as a discharge, *pro tanto*, of the creditor's judgment; and that judgment being thus satisfied, there could be no substitution."[2] The quotation we have just made, very fairly represents the reasoning of those courts, which hold that the purchaser at a void execution or judicial sale cannot be subrogated to the rights of the holder of the lien which his payment has contributed to discharge. It must be confessed that the reasoning is in consonance with the general law of subrogation. This general law affords no encouragement to one person, who voluntarily discharges the debt of another. Such a person is styled a volunteer. His acts are without compulsion, and he is, therefore, not classed with those persons who are compelled, as sureties or other-

---

[1] 1 Leading Cases in Equity, 113, and authorities there cited.
[2] Richmond v. Marston, 15 Ind. 136; s. c., 42 Am. Dec. 201.

wise, to discharge obligations on which others are primarily responsible. The purchaser at a void judicial sale acts under a mistake of law; and this, as is well known, is rarely, if ever, recognized as sufficient to induce the interposition of courts of equity. Purchasers at void probate sales have also been judged not to be entitled to subrogation to the rights of the creditors whose claims their purchases had discharged,[1] but the right of purchasers at a void judicial sale, whether in probate or chancery to subrogation, is steadily gaining ground, and is now established by the decided preponderance of authority, as will appear from the following sections.

§ 52. **Right of Purchasers at Execution and Chancery Sales to Subrogation, Affirmed.**—We pass now to the authorities in conflict with those cited in the preceding section. From these authorities it will be seen that the right of purchasers at void sales, to be subrogated to the claims they have discharged by their payments, is very generally recognized in this country. In Kentucky, a slave named Jack, was sold under execution against an estate, and was purchased by Enos Daniel. The slave was subsequently recovered from Daniel in an action of *detinue*, under a title paramount to that of the decedent. Daniel then commenced a suit in chancery to be subrogated to the rights of the holder of the judgment under which the sale had been made. The case was, therefore, one in which the title had failed, not from any defect in the sale or judgment, but because the defendant in execution was not the owner of the property. The court, nevertheless, sustained the claim for subrogation, saying: "Admitting that Enos Daniel knew that Jack belonged to Mary McLaughlin, and was not subject to execution against the estate, this, in our judgment, presents no legal impediment to his claim upon the estate

---

[1] Nowler v. Coit, 1 Oh. 236; s. c., 13 Am. Dec. 640; Salmond v. Price, 13 Oh. 368; Lieb v. Ludlow, 4 Oh. 469; s. c., Bishop v. O'Conner, 69 Ill. 431. The rule in this State has been changed by statute.

for the amount of Clark's demand paid by him. The slave was sold as the property of the estate, under the process of law; he purchased him, and by his purchase and execution of a sale-bond to Clark, he satisfied and extinguished that amount against the estate, and for which it stood responsible. And, according to the principle repeatedly recognized in this court, he has an equitable right to be substituted in place of the creditor, and to have the amount so paid refunded to him out of the estate. His equity rests, not upon the ground of his want of knowledge as to the title of the slave, but on the ground of his having discharged a judgment against the estate, for which it stood chargeable, by a purchase of property made under the coercive process of the law; and, therefore, has equitable right to be reimbursed out of the estate."[1] In South Carolina, a plaintiff, at his own sale, purchased the interest of the defendant in certain personal property. There were older writs in the hands of the officer making the sale, and the proceeds were exclusively applied to those writs. The sale turned out to be void. The plaintiff's judgment was subsequently paid; but he was not repaid the purchase money, which had been applied to the extinction of older claims. In these circumstances, it was held that his "claim is that of a junior creditor, who has paid prior debts, and he must be substituted in the place of the senior creditors, and subrogated to all their rights."[2] In Louisiana and Texas, if an execution sale is void for some irregularity of proceeding, but is made under a valid judgment, and the proceeds of the sale are applied to the satisfaction of the judgment, the defendant cannot recover the property from the purchaser without first repaying the amount paid at the sale.[3] When a void sale is made under proceedings to foreclose a mortgage,

---

[1] McLaughlin v. Daniel, 8 Dana, 183.
[2] Bentley v. Long, 1 Strob. Eq. 52; s. c., 47 Am. Dec. 523.
[3] Howard v. North, 5 Tex. 316; s. c., 51 Am. Dec. 769; Dufour v. Camfranc, 11 Mart. 610; s. c., 13 Am. Dec. 369.

there seems to be no doubt that the purchaser succeeds to the title and rights of the mortgagee, and may enforce them as the mortgagee could have done, but for the sale.[1]

§ 53. **Right to Subrogation Affirmed in Favor of Purchasers at Probate Sales.**—The cases in which the equitable rule of subrogation has been most frequently invoked with success, have arisen under sales made by administrators, executors and guardians. Thus, in North Carolina, a bill in equity was filed, showing that a sale of lands had been made to plaintiff by the defendant, as executor; that in a trial at law the sale had been declared void for want of authority in the executor to sell; that the purchase money has been paid to the defendant; that $108 of this money remained in the hands of the executor, and the balance thereof had been applied to the payment of the debts of the testator. The bill prayed that the $108 be refunded, and that as to the balance of the purchase money, the plaintiff might stand in the place of the creditors whose claims it had satisfied, and that the land be sold for the payment thereof. The following is from the opinion of the court: "The claim of the plaintiff's to be substituted to the creditors, whose demands they have satisfied, is supported, we think, by well settled principles. By the laws of this State, real as well as personal property is liable for debts of every description; but personal property is the primary fund for their satisfaction. It is alleged that the personal assets were insufficient for the discharge of all the debts. Whether this be the fact or not, can only be ascertained by taking an account of the assets and of the administration of them. If, in taking the account, the fact should be established as alleged, then it follows, from the doctrine sanctioned in the cases of Williams v. Williams,[2] and Saunders v. Saunders,[3]

---

[1] Brobst v. Brock, 10 Wall. 519; Jackson v. Bowen, 7 Cow. 13; Gilbert v. Cooley, Walker's Ch. 494.

[2] 2 Dev. Eq. 69; s. c., 22 A. D. 729.

[3] 2 Dev. Eq. 262.

that the defendant Dunn would have a right in a court of equity to be subrogated to those creditors who have been paid by his advances. As between Dunn and the plaintiff, if their money were yet in his hands he could not retain it with a safe conscience, and would be obliged to refund it. And it seems to us clear, that if he could rightfully reclaim it from his co-defendants, he might be compelled to assert this right, or permit the plaintiffs to assert it in his name, in order that it might be refunded. The court would do this upon the same principle by which the surety, on making satisfaction to the creditor, becomes entitled to demand every means of enforcing payment which the creditor himself had against the principal debtor; a principle which, when traced to its origin, is founded on the plain obligations of humanity, which bind every one to furnish to another those aids to escape from loss which he can part with without injury to himself. * * * The doctrine of substitution, which prevails in equity, is not founded on contract, but, as we have seen, on the principles of natural justice. Unquestionably, the devisees are not to be injured by the mistake of the executor, as to the extent of his power over their land; but that mistake should not give them unfair gains. The executor was not an officious intermedler in paying off the debts of the testator, and his erroneous belief that he could indemnify himself in a particular way, should not bar him from obtaining indemnity by legitimate means. It is not a question here, whether a mistake of law shall confer any rights, but whether such a mistake shall be visited with a forfeiture of rights wholly independent of that mistake." [1]

In the case of Valle v. Fleming's Heirs,[2] a void administrator's sale had been made, and the proceeds thereof applied to the payment of a mortgage existing on the lands sold.

---

[1] Scott v. Dunn, 1 Dev. & Bat. Eq. 427; s. c., 30 Am. Dec. 174, and note.
[2] 29 Mo. 152; s. c., 77 Am. Dec. —.

Ejectment was subsequently brought, to which the purchasers filed an equitable defense, and prayed to be subrogated to the rights of the mortgagees. Judge Napton, in delivering the opinion of the court, referred to the equity maxims, both of the common and of the civil law, as well as to the decisions of the American courts, and concluded as follows: "Nothing could be more unjust, we may repeat, than to permit a person to sell a tract of land and take the purchase money, and then, because the sale happens to be informal and void, to allow him, or, which is the same thing, his heir, to recover back the land and keep the money. Any code of law which would tolerate this would seem to be liable to the reproach of being a very imperfect, or a very inequitable one. We think that, upon well established principles of equity law, the owner of the land should, if he wishes to get it back, repay the purchase money which he has received, or which he will receive if he gets the land. This may be done upon the compensation doctrine of courts of equity, with which, as it is settled on all hands, it is not inconsistent, if we regard the claim of the owner under such circumstances, as the Roman law treated it, as a case of fraud or ill faith. But whether this equity be administered under the name of compensation, or by substituting the purchaser in the place of the creditors whose debts he has paid, or by giving him the benefit of the mortgage which his money has paid off, is not material. The answer put in by the defendants should not have been stricken out, and in order that the answer may be reinstated, and the case may be tried upon these equitable principles, the judgment is reversed, and the case will be remanded." [1]

---

[1] Valle's Heirs v. Fleming's Heirs, 29 Mo. 164; s. c., 77 Am. Dec. —. Judge Scott dissented in a vigorous and well written opinion, saying, among other things: "The defendants are volunteers and strangers in relation to the plaintiffs. No man can make another his debtor without his consent. Nor can any man pay a debt of another without his authority, and claim it of him. This is an important principle necessary to be

Nor is the claim to subrogation confined to those cases where a mortgage or some other record lien has been paid off by the sale. The estates of deceased persons are liable to be sold for the payment of the debts of the decedents, whether such debts are liens or not. If, by a sale of the lands of a decedent, his debts are paid, and it turns out that the sale is void, the purchaser has the right to be subrogated to the claims which he has, by his purchase, paid; and he has also the right to retain possession of the property as security for the repayment of the sums to which he is entitled.

The case of Blodgett v. Hitt,[1] discusses more thoroughly than any other with which we are familiar the rights of purchasers under void probate sales. We copy so much of the opinion of the court as is devoted to this subject: "The evidence on this subject is, that the defendant bid off the land at the administrator's sale for $365; that out of this sum he paid the Boyd mortgage, amounting to nearly $250, and that he paid the balance of the purchase money to the administrator. The whole of the purchase money was applied to the payment of the mortgage, of other debts against the estate, and of the expenses of administration. The land in question stood chargeable with the payment of such mortgage debts and expenses. The payments made by the defendant, on account of his purchase, enured to the benefit of the owners of the land. There is no manner of doubt but the defendant purchased the land, and paid his money therefor, in perfectly good faith, supposing that he was obtaining the whole title thereto; and there is no pretense that he had any actual notice of the defect in the proceedings before the sale, which invalidates his title. The question then is, whether, under such circumstances, the defendant is entitled to be repaid the money which he has paid preserved, and it is one which has had its influence in all cases in which it has been involved."

[1] 29 Wis. 182.

in good faith to relieve the land from incumbrances, before he can be turned out of possession thereof. Suppose, for illustration, that the liabilities against the estate of Pearley P. Blodgett, after the personal estate was exhausted, were just $365, for the payment of which the land, which the administrator attempted to convey to the defendant, was chargeable. The interest of the heirs of Blodgett in the land was precisely that sum less than a full and perfect title thereto. That is to say, the creditors of the intestate owned an equitable interest therein to the amount of $365, and the heirs were the owners of the residue. Now, when the defendant, supposing in good faith that he was thereby obtaining a title to the lands, paid those debts and took a conveyance of the land from the administrator, and when it turns out that, by reason of the failure of the administrator to perform and fulfill an essential prerequisite to a valid sale, the defendant gets no title by such conveyance, and the heirs recover the land, it must be admitted that there is no justice in giving the land to heirs, cleared of the incumbrances which the defendant has paid, without requiring them to repay the sums thus paid by him for their benefit. Otherwise, the heirs would recover a greater interest in the land than they inherited, by the sum of $365, and the defendant would be out of pocket to that amount, paid by him for their benefit. The fact that the purchase money, paid by the defendant, only cancelled a small percentage of the indebtedness against the estate, does not change the principle. But the question is not alone—what is the natural and inherent justice of the case? but it is—are the principles and rules of equity jurisprudence, as recognized and enforced by courts of equity, sufficiently broad and comprehensive to reach the case and compel the heirs to repay the sums which the defendant has thus paid for their benefit, before they will be permitted to take possession of the land in controversy? We are of the opinion that this latter question must be answered in the affirmative, both upon principle and by authority. A brief reference will be made to a few of the leading cases, wherein it has been so held.

"Hudgin v. Hudgin,[1] was a case where a person, by will, charged his lands with the payment of his debts. After his death, a creditor procured an order from the proper court for the sale of some portion of the lands thus made chargeable with the debts of the testator. The lands were sold, and the proceeds applied to the payment of such debts. The sale and conveyance, executed pursuant thereto, were subsequently held void, and, in ejectment brought by some of the devisees of the land against the purchaser at such sale, or the person claiming under him, the devisee recovered judgment. The defendant in the ejectment, filed his bill in equity and obtained an injunction, restraining proceedings upon such judgment, and, upon proof of these facts, the court of appeals of Virginia directed a decree declaring the purchase money, so paid by the complainant, or his grantor, on such void sale, and the interest thereon, after deducting therefrom the rents and profits of the land while occupied by the purchaser or his grantee (exclusive of improvements made by them respectively), to be a charge on the land, and providing that, unless the same should be paid by the devisees within a reasonable time, the land be sold for the satisfaction thereof, on terms to be prescribed for the purpose. This case is decided upon the principles that the purchaser, whose money has paid the incumbrances upon the land, has the right to be substituted to the rights of the creditor whose debt he has paid; and, because equity will not permit such creditor or incumbrancer, lawfully in possession, to be disturbed therein until his debt or incumbrance is fully satisfied, it will not permit such purchaser, who has paid the incumbrance in good faith, and is thereby subrogated to the rights of the

[1] 6 Grat. 320; s. c., 52 Am. Dec. 124.

creditor, to be dispossessd until he is reimbursed for the moneys so paid by him.

"Valle's Heirs v. Fleming's Heirs,[1] is to the same effect. This is a very important and interesting case, and will justify a somewhat extended notice. The action was in the nature of ejectment. The plaintiffs claimed, as heirs of Valle, who died, seized of the lands in controversy in the action. The defendants were in possession under certain conveyances, executed to their ancestor and his grantors by the administrators of the estate of Valle, pursuant to a sale of the land under an order of the proper court. In a former litigation these conveyances had been adjudged to be null and void by the supreme court of Missouri. In their answer the defendants alleged, as an equitable defense and counter-claim, that their ancestor and his grantors purchased the lands in good faith, and paid therefor $50,000, which moneys the administrators applied to the payment and satisfaction of a mortgage upon said lands, and, perhaps, other lands of which Valle died siezed. The defendants claimed that, notwithstanding the apparent and technical payment and extinguishment of such mortgage, equity would, under the circumstances, treat it as still subsisting and unsatisfied, for the protection of the purchasers from the administrators, or their grantees, and would subrogate such purchasers or grantees to all of the rights of the mortgagee, treating them as assignees and purchasers of the mortgage, for a valuable consideration by them paid. They also claimed that they were, in fact and in equity, in possession of the land in controversy as assigns of said mortgage, and fully entitled to set up the same against any person attacking their rights or possession thereto. The court below rejected these views of the case, and struck out from the answer such equitable defense and counter-claim; but the supreme court reversed the judgment below for that

---

[1] 29 Mo. 152; s. c., 77 Am. Dec. —.

reason, and in a very able opinion by Judge Napton, a majority of the court fully sustain the theory of the defendants, and they were entitled to the equitable protection of the court as mortgagees in possession under an unpaid mortgage, and that their possession could not be disturbed until an account should be taken and the sum ascertained to be equitably due to them on the mortgage fully paid. In that case Judge Scott, delivered a dissenting opinion, wherein he claims that the views of the majority of the court are unsustained by the cases; that the decision creates a new equity, or rather injects a new principle into the equity jurisprudence of the country; and, further, that the defendant's ancestor and his grantors, who paid their money under a void sale and conveyance, were mere volunteers; and, because a man may not pay the debt of another without his authority and claim it of him, the learned judge concludes that, the defendants (who had succeeded to all of the rights of the original purchasers) could not be subrogated to the rights of the mortgagee, and recover of the heirs, or out of the land, the money which was thus voluntarily paid on a void conveyance. It is believed that both these positions are untenable. That this is no new equity—one first recognized and asserted in that case—is abundantly shown by a reference to the cases cited in the majority opinion. Some of those cases will be hereinafter mentioned. Again, the lands having been purchased of the administrator in good faith, and at a sale which had been ordered to be made by the proper court, and the purchasers having paid a valuable consideration for the land, in the belief that they were obtaining a good title thereto, it cannot be said, in any reasonable or just sense, that they were mere volunteers. On the contrary, they paid their money at the request and by the procurement of the administrators; and, inasmuch as the administrators were charged by law with the duty of converting the assets and paying the debt, it may well be held that they were the representatives

of the heirs, to the extent that the latter should be held
bound by such request, and should not be heard to allege
that the purchasers, whose money went to pay the incumbrance upon the land, were mere volunteers. The judge
also speaks of the distinction between trusts and powers,
and says that because the administrators have nothing but
a mere power, without an interest, the land cannot be
affected by their conveyance thereof, unless the power is
executed pursuant to the terms of the statute by which it is
conferred. In this the learned judge is doubtless correct,
as he would have been had he said further, that where, as
in that case, a power is created by law, equity will not
relieve against a defective execution of it. But the result of
these principles is not that a purchaser in good faith at an
administrator's sale is not entitled, in a case where the
conveyance to him has been adjudged void, to be repaid
by the heir, or out of the land, the money paid by him for
such void conveyance, and applied in payment and satisfaction of incumbrances upon the estate, but only that the
power having been defectively executed, the conveyance is
void, and a court of equity has no jurisdiction or authority
to heal the defect and make it valid.

"The foregoing case was decided mainly upon the authority of the case of Bright v. Boyd.[1] This is, perhaps, the
leading case on the question under consideration. Boyd,
the defendant, had recovered judgment, in an action of
ejectment, for certain premises in the possession of Bright,
the complainant; whereupon Bright filed his bill in equity
against Boyd, alleging that he was in possession of the
premises in controversy, by intermediate conveyances from
the administrator, with the will annexed of the estate of
John P. Boyd, the father of defendant, but that the title
under the administrator's deed had failed, or rather that
the same conveyed no title by reason of the failure of the

---

[1] 1 Story, 478, and 2 Ib. 605.

administrator to comply with certain requirements of the law, which were held to be essential to the validity of the sale; and that the complainant, or those under whom he claimed in good faith, and believing that the deed from the administrator conveyed a good title to the premises, had made valuable and permanent improvements thereon. The object of the bill was to make the value of such improvements a charge upon, and to enforce payment therefor out of the premises which the defendant had recovered in the ejectment suit. The defendant, Boyd, made title to the land as devised under the will of his father. On proof of these allegations, Justice Story, before whom the cause was heard, after great deliberation and research, gave the complainant the relief prayed in the bill, and, in the absence of any statutory provision on the subject, held the broad doctrine that, ' a *bona fide* purchaser for a valuable consideration, without notice of any defect in his title, who makes improvements and meliorations upon the estate, has a lien or charge thereupon for the increased value, which is thereby given to the estate beyond its value without them, and a court of equity will enforce the lien or charge against the true owner, who recovers the estate in a suit at law against the purchaser.'

"The principle there asserted is precisely the same as that involved in the question under consideration in this case. In both cases, if the land is held chargeable, it is because the money of the purchaser under the void sale has been paid in good faith, and expended to increase the value of the estate. It is quite immaterial whether this was done by paying off incumbrances, or by making permanent and valuable improvements. In either case, the value of the inheritance is increased by the expenditure, and, as already observed, the plainest principles of justice demand that the heir or devisee should repay the money thus innocently expended for his benefit, to the extent that he has been benefitted thereby. The opinion of Judge Story, in Bright

v. Boyd, is exceedingly learned and able, and will well repay careful perusal and study. He traces the principle which he applied there to the Roman law, and shows that it has been adopted into the laws of all modern nations which derive their jurisprudence from the Roman law, and demonstrates, by reference to the writings of Cujacius, Pothier, Grotius, Bell, Puffendorf, Rutherforth and others, and by arguments which seem conclusive of the question, that 'such principle has the highest and most persuasive equity, as well as common sense and common justice, for its foundation.' We are not aware that the authority of that case has ever been shaken, or its correctness ever successfully assailed.

"Before dismissing the case of Bright v. Boyd from our consideration, I may be permitted to transcribe a passage from the opinion, to show how identical in principle that case is with the present one, and also to show the views of the eminent jurist who wrote the opinion upon the precise question involved in this case. Judge Story there says that 'it cannot be overlooked that the lands of the testator now in controversy were sold for the payment of his just debts, under the authority of law, although the authority was not regularly executed by the administrator in his mode of sale, by a non-compliance with one of the prerequisites. It was not, therefore, in a just sense, a tortious sale; and the proceeds thereof, paid by the purchaser, have gone to discharge the debts of the testator, and, so far, the lands in the hands of the defendant (Boyd) have been relieved from a charge to which they were liable by law. So that he is now enjoying the lands free from a charge which, in conscience and equity, he, and he only, and not the purchaser, it seems to me that plaintiff, claiming under the purchaser, is entitled to reimbursement, in order to avoid circuity of action, to get back the money from the administrator, and thus subject the lands to a new sale, or, at least, in his favor, in equity to the old charge. I confess myself to be unwilling to resort to such a circuity in order to do justice, where, upon the principles of equity, the merits of the case can be reached by affecting the lands directly with a charge to which they are *ex æquo et bono* in the hands of the present defendant, clearly liable.[1]

"After what has been already said, concerning the rule of the civil law on this subject, we should expect to find the courts of Louisiana asserting and enforcing that rule. Accordingly, we find, in Dufour v. Camfranc,[2] the following language: 'It has been proved that the proceeds arising from the sale of the slaves were applied to the discharge of the judgment debts of the plaintiff, and the courts are of opinion that he cannot recover in the suit until he repay that money. * * * Nothing could be more unjust than to permit a debtor to recover back his property because the sale was irregular, and yet allow him to profit by that irregular sale to pay his debts.' It will be readily inferred from the foregoing extracts, that the action was brought to recover certain slaves, which the defendant had purchased at a sheriff's sale upon an execution, which sale, it was afterwards held, was void and transferred no title to the slaves to the purchaser, but the proceeds of the sale went to pay judgment debts against the plaintiff. * * * We hold, therefore, that the whole purchase money, paid by the defendant for the land in controversy, and the interest thereon, less the *mesne* profits of the land (exclusive of the improvements placed thereon by him) during his occupancy thereof, is a lien and charge upon the land, and that the plaintiffs cannot have restitution of the land claimed by them until the amount of such lien and charge is paid."[3]

---

[1] 1 Story, 193.
[2] 11 Martin, 607, (2 Cond. La. Reports, 234); s. c., 13 Am. Dec. 364.
[3] Blodgett v. Hitt, 29 Wis. 182. The following cases are in harmony with the one just cited: Bright v. Boyd, 2 Story C. C. 605; Mohr v.

The more recent decisions have been in favor of recognizing and enforcing the claims of purchasers at void sales, by whose purchase moneys have been realized, and when realized have been applied in payment of liens upon the property purchased, or of claims which, though not secured by any specific lien, were enforceable against the assets of the estate, and for the payment of which the lands in controversy might have been sold. The heirs will not be permitted to recover the property unless they reimburse the purchaser for the moneys paid by him, and which have benefitted them by discharging claims against the estate.[1]

Tulip, 40 Wis. 66; Grant v. Loyd, 12 S. & M. 191; Levy v. Riley, 4 Org. 392; Short v. Porter, 44 Miss. 533; Williamson v. Williamson, 3 S. & M. 715; s. c., 41 Am. Dec. 636; Douglass v. Bennett, 51 Miss. 680; Hudgin v. Hudgin, 6 Gratt. 320; s. c., 52 Am. Dec. 124; Winslow v. Crowell, 32 Wis. 639; Dunbar v. Creditors, 2 La. An. 727; Stockton v. Downey, 6 La. An. 581; Ragland v. Green, 14 S. & M. 194. "If the sale be void or voidable, the lien of the administrator continues; and it would seem equitable that the purchaser, who has paid the debts of the estate, should have a lien on the estate for his purchase money." Haynes v. Meeks, 10 Cal. 110; s. c., 70 Am. Dec. 703. A purchaser has no claim against the heirs nor their estate for purchase money which he fails to show has been applied for their benefit. Jayne v. Boisgerard, 39 Miss. 796. In Illinois, if application is made to a court of equity to set aside a sale, the relief will not be granted, unless the complainants do equity on their part, and refund so much of the purchase money as may have come into their possession. Chambers v. Jones, 72 Ill. 275. If the money paid by the purchaser has been applied to the extinguishment of liens on the property purchased, he is entitled to be subrogated to such liens. Kinney v. Knoebel, 51 Ill. 112. But where, in a probate sale, the money is paid to discharge debts not secured by any specific lien, the purchaser is without redress. Bishop v. O'Conner, 51 Ill. 437.

[1] Schaefer v. Causey, 8 Mo. App. 142; s. c., 76 Mo. 365; Jones v. Manly, 58 Mo. 559; Evans v. Snyder, 64 Mo. 517; Sharky v. Bankston, 30 La. An. 891; Hatcher v. Briggs, 6 Org. 31; Sands v. Lynham, 27 Gratt. 291; s. c., 21 Am. Rep. 348; Snider v. Coleman, 72 Mo. 568; Davis v. Gaines, 104 U. S. 386; Barrelli v. Ganche, 24 La. An. 324; Gaines v. Kennedy, 53 Miss. 103; Hill v. Billingsly, 53 Miss. 111; McGee v. Wallis, 57 Miss. 638; Jouet v. Mortimer, 29 La. An. 207; Davidson v. Davidson, 28 La. An. 269; Bland v. Bowel, 53 Ala. 152; Goodman v. Winter, 64 Ala. 410; Robertson v. Bradford, 73 Ala. 116.

§ 54. Right to Subrogation, When Purchaser is Guilty of Fraud.—It is a familiar principle, that whoever seeks equity must come with clean hands. Nearly all the cases in which relief has been granted to purchasers at void sales, have proceeded upon the express ground that the purchaser had acted in good faith, and in ignorance of the irregularity by which his title was impaired. Certainly in all such cases the purchaser's good faith ought to be regarded as material. In Pennsylvania, if a purchaser be guilty of a fraud, on account of which his purchase is adjudged void, he cannot reclaim his purchase money. He, in effect, forfeits it to those whom he sought to defraud, for they may retain the money and recover the estate.[1] In Mississippi, on the other hand, a fraudulent purchaser may assert the same equities as one who has acted in good faith.[2]

§ 55. Purchaser's Right to the Aid of Equity in Supplying Omissions and Mistakes.—In every case where a purchaser has, in good faith, made and complied with his bid, his equities are of a very persuasive character, and usually appeal to our sense of justice more strongly than the equities of him who seeks to avoid the sale without placing the purchaser in *statu quo*. In many cases, it is apparent that the vice which renders the sale a nullity has not, in fact, operated to the detriment of him whose property was sold. All the parties may have supposed the proceedings to be regular; the biddings may have been spirited; the price realized may have equalled, or, perhaps, exceeded the value of the property; the proceeds of the sale may have all been applied in the manner directed by law, and still some act or omission, unnoticed at the time, may render the purchaser's title utterly void at law. In such a case, our sense of justice revolts at the thought that he may

---

[1] McCaskey v. Graff, 23 Pa. St. 321; s. c., 62 Am. Dec. 336; Gilbert v. Hoffman, 2 Watts, 66; s. c., 26 Am. Dec. 103; Jackson v. Summerville, 13 Pa. St. 359.

[2] Grant v. Loyd, 12 S. & M. 191.

be without redress. We naturally expect that equity will interpose to supply the omission, or that, on such terms as may be just, it will enjoin the parties in interest from availing themselves of an error which clearly has not impaired their rights. But, on seeking relief, we are at once confronted with the reminder that, "in cases of defective execution of powers, we are carefully to distinguish between powers which are created by private parties and those which are specially created by statute; as, for instance, powers of tenants in tail to make leases. The latter are construed with more strictness, and, whatever formalities are required by the statute, must be punctually complied with, otherwise the defect cannot be helped, or, at least, may not, perhaps, be helped in equity, for courts of equity cannot dispense with the regulations prescribed by statute, at least where they constitute the apparent policy and object of the statute."[1] Perhaps this language, owing to the author's timidity of expression, may not necessarily dispose of the purchaser's claim for relief. The other authorities are more decisive, especially with regard to execution, judicial and probate sales. Thus, in a case decided by Judge Story, it appeared that an administrator's sale had been regularly licensed, and that all the requirements of the statute had been respected, save that requiring a bond to be given and approved prior to the sale. The judge, in his opinion, said: "Upon this case, coming out on the trial of the action at law (a writ of entry), the court held that the giving of the bond was, by law, an essential prerequisite to the sale; and, it not having been complied with, the sale was consequently valid and passed no title to the purchaser. It is now argued that however correct this doctrine may be at law, yet, in a court of equity, the omis-

---

[1] Story's Eq. Jur. sec. 96. See Ib., sec. 177; 1 Lead. Cas. in Eq., 4th Am. Ed. 379; Freeman on Executions, sec. 332; Tiernan v. Beam, 2 Oh. 465; s. c., 15 Am. Dec. 557; Ware v. Johnson, 55 Mo. 500; Moreau v. Branham, 27 Mo. 351; McBryde v. Wilkinson, 29 Ala. 662.

sion to give the bond, within a stipulated time, ought not to be held a fatal defect, but it should be treated as a mistake, or inadvertence, or accident properly remediable in a court of equity. We do not think so. The mistake was a voluntary omission, or neglect of duty, and in no just sense an accident. But, if it were otherwise, it would be difficult, in the present case, to sustain the argument. This is not the case of the defective execution of a power created by the testator himself, but of a power, created and regulated by statute. Now it is a well settled doctrine that, although courts of equity may relieve against the defective execution of a power created by a party, yet they cannot relieve against the defective execution of a power created by law, or dispense with any of the formalities required thereby for its due execution; for, otherwise, the whole policy of the legislative enactments might be overturned. There may, perhaps, be exceptions to this rule, but if there be the present case does not present any circumstances which ought to take it out of the general rule. Therefore, it seems to us that the non-compliance with the statute prerequisites, in the present case, is equally fatal in equity as it is in law." [1]

In Illinois, certain heirs recovered a judgment in ejectment for lands purchased at a guardian's sale. The defect in the purchaser's title was the omission of the guardian to report the proceedings under the order of sale. The purchaser then filed a bill to enjoin the execution of the judgment in ejectment, and for general relief. The supreme court decided that the bill must be dismissed. Caton, J., in delivering the opinion of the court, considered and approved the views expressed by Judge Story in his Commentaries, and also in Bright v. Boyd, both of which have been quoted in this section. He further said: "If chancery may interfere and dispense with one of the requirements of the statute it may with another, and thus in its unlimited dis-

[1] Bright v. Boyd, 1 Story C. C. 486.

cretion it may fritter away the whole statute. It is seriously claimed that, because the purchaser purchased in good faith, and paid the full value of the property to the guardian of the owners, thereby an equity is raised in his favor and against them, which the court will enforce. Equities do not arise upon statutory acts without the volition of those against whom the equity is charged. Suppose this guardian, seeing that a case existed which would require the circuit court to order a sale of the infant's estate, and, in ignorance of the law, but in all honesty, had sold the estate for its full value, and without an order of court, to a purchaser who, in good faith, supposed he was getting a good title, in that case the purchaser's equity would be just as strong as in the equity in this case; and, should we now hold that the purchaser here acquired an equitable title, which should be enforced against the heir, it would be equally our duty, when the supposed case arises, to compel a conveyance to the purchaser, and then the entire statute would be gone. But the truth is, the purchaser at these statutory sales gets no imperfect equitable title which may be perfected in chancery; he gets the whole title which the infant had, or he gets no title whatever." [1]

As equity will not supply an act omitted inadvertently or otherwise, so it will not correct a mere mistake, nor relieve the purchaser from the consequences of a mistake. Thus, if by mistake part of a tract intended to be embraced in an order of sale is omitted therefrom, or if a tract altogether different from the one intended, is inserted therein, and the error passes unnoticed until after the sale, equity cannot relieve the purchaser, nor give him the tract which he supposed he was buying, and which the administrator or other officer intended to sell.[2] In Iowa, this rule seems to

---

[1] Young v. Dowling, 15 Ill. 481, 485.
[2] Dickey v. Beatty, 14 Oh. St. 389; Mahan v. Reeve, 6 Blackf. 215; Ward v. Brewer, 19 Ill. 291; Rogers v. Abbott, 37 Ind. 138; Runnels v. Kaylor, 95 Ind. 503; Keepfer v. Force, 86 Ind. 81.

be ignored. A judgment was entered in that State for the sale of a part of several lots of land. From the execution and other proceedings subsequent to judgment, one of these lots was omitted. After the sale and delivery of the deed, the purchaser discovered the omission. By a proceeding in equity, he succeeded in setting aside the sale and the satisfaction of the judgment thereby produced, and obtained leave to issue a new execution in conformity with his judgment.[1] This case, it will be seen, did not validate a void sale. It did, however, give relief, which ultimately proved as effectual; for it gave the right to make a sale of property which had not been sold at all. Where a mistake, made in describing property in a mortgage, has been carried into the proceedings for foreclosure, so that a piece of land has been throughout improperly designated, the mortgagee is not without redress. He may, notwithstanding the judgment and sale, at least where he is the purchaser, maintain an action to reform the mortgage, and to foreclose it as reformed. The technical objection to this proceeding is, that the mortgage has already became merged in the judgment of foreclosure, and no longer exists for the purpose of being reformed. To this objection, this reply is generally made: "The reformed mortgage is not merged in any decree, for there is no decree for the sale of any premises described in the mortgage, as corrected and reformed. The decree may be satisfied at least *pro tanto* to the amount of the sale; but the decree was based on the mistaken, and not the true, mortgage; the sale was of land not embraced in the true mortgage; no money or other valuable thing was ever received by plaintiff; the whole proceeding is infected by the original mistake, and is, therefore, baseless, unsubstantial and nugatory."[2] Relief will be granted against all persons claiming under the mortgagor, who do not stand in the

---

[1] Snyder v. Ives, 42 Ia. 157.
[2] Davenport v. Sovil, 6 Oh. St. 465; Conyers v. Mericles, 75 Ind. 443; State Bank v. Abbott, 20 Wis. 599; Blodgett v. Hobart, 18 Vt. 414.

position of purchasers or incumbrancers in good faith, for value, and without notice.[1] Where some person other than the mortgagee has become the purchaser under the foreclosure, we presume his remedy must be by a suit seeking to be subrogated to the mortgagee's right to have the mortgage reformed and foreclosed, according to the description intended by the parties. It seems certain that such purchaser cannot reform the mortgage, the decree of foreclosure and sheriff's deed in one suit;[2] and while he has equities of a very high character, they certainly do not entitle him to treat his purchase as a complete and binding acquisition of lands which have never been ordered sold, which no officer had any authority to sell, and which, therefore, could never have induced that competition among intending bidders which would have attended a sale by a proper description and based on unquestionable authority.

While equity will not usually aid the defective execution of a statutory power, we judge that this rule cannot prevail where all the prerequisites prescribed by law have been observed, but the purchaser has either received no conveyance or one which is not such as he is entitled to receive. In this case, the parties whose property was sold will be enjoined from availing themselves of the omission,[3] or the officer will be compelled to perform his duty by executing a conveyance in proper form.[4]

---

[1] Strang v. Beach, 11 Oh. St. 283.

[2] Miller v. Kolb, 47 Ind. 220; Lewis v. Owen, 64 Ind. 446; Angle v. Spear, 66 Ind. 488.

[3] Wortman v. Skinner, 1 Beas. 358; De Riemer v. De Cantillon, 4 Johns. Ch. 85.

[4] Jelks v. Barrett, 52 Miss. 315; Stewart v. Stokes, 33 Ala. 494; Freeman on Executions, sec. 332. Probably a sheriff's deed may be reformed in equity in Indiana and New York. Johns v. DeRome, 5 Blackf. 421; Bartlett v. Judd, 21 N. Y. 200. Deeds of commissioners and administrators may, in certain cases, be reformed by equitable action in Missouri. Houx v. County of Bates, 61 Mo. 391; Grayson v. Weddle, 63 Mo. 523.

CHAPTER VI.

THE CONSTITUTIONALITY OF CURATIVE STATUTES.

SECTION.
- 56. Curative Statutes Upheld by Supreme Court of United States.
- 57. Curative Statutes Confirming Irregular Judicial Proceedings.
- 58. Curative Statutes Confirming Void Judicial Proceedings.
- 59. Defects, other than Jurisdictional, which are Pronounced Incurable.
- 60. Informalities which may be Waived by Subsequent Statutes.
- 61. Limitation on Effect of Curative Statutes.
- 62. General Reflection Concerning Curative Statutes.

§ 56. **Curative Statutes Upheld by Supreme Court of United States.**—Numerous statutes have been enacted, professing to validate judicial sales and proceedings which, without the aid of such statutes, were unquestionably inoperative, both at law and in equity. Such statutes are clearly retrospective. They also take, at least, the legal title away from its owner, and vest it in another person without due process of law. They usually, if not universally, do even more than this, for they give force to titles which are not less void in equity than at law. They have, therefore, been questioned as conflicting with express constitutional provisions, and also as violating some principles which, even without any direct constitutional expressions, must be admittted to prevail under every civilized form of government.[1]

[1] For an annunciation of the rule that there must necessarily be some restraints upon legislative authority in every free and civilized country,

We shall first call attention to a case which, as it arose in a State then having no constitution, may, perhaps, be accepted as an authoritative determination of this question, where it is to be answered solely from the constitution of the United States, as that instrument stood before the adoption of the fourteenth amendment. Jonathan Jenckes died in New Hampshire, leaving a will which was there admitted to probate. The executrix obtained a license of the judge of probate in New Hampshire, purporting to authorize her to sell lands in Rhode Island. Under this license, she sold and conveyed lands in the last named State. The sale was confessedly void, because the courts of New Hampshire had no jurisdiction over lands situate in another State. She made an application to the legislature of Rhode Island, stating the facts in her petition, and thereupon an act was passed at the June session of 1792, ratifying and confirming the title based on her sales and conveyances.

In determining the constitutionality of this act, Mr. Justice Story, delivering the opinion of the supreme court of the United States, said: "Rhode Island is the only State in the union which has not a written constitution of government, containing its fundamental laws and institutions. Until the revolution of 1776 it was governed by the charter granted by Charles II., in the fifteenth year of his reign. That charter has ever since continued in its general provisions to regulate the exercise and distribution of the powers of government. It has never been formally abrogated by the people, and, except so far as it has been modified to meet the exigencies of the revolution, may be considered as now a fundamental law. By this charter the power to make laws is granted to the general assembly in the most complete manner, 'so as such laws, etc., be not contrary and repugnant unto, but as near as may be agree-

---

independent of direct constitutional prohibitions and assurances, see Calder v. Bull, 3 Dall. 386; Wilkinson v. Leland, 2 Pet. 656; Loan Association v. Topeka, 20 Wall. 663; Story on the Const., sec. 1399.

able to the laws, etc., of England, considering the nature and constitution of the place and people there.' What is the true extent of the power thus granted, must be open to explanation, as well by usage as by construction of the terms in which it is given. In a government professing to regard the great rights of personal liberty and of property, and which is required to legislate in subordination to the general laws of England, it would not lightly be presumed that the great principles of Magna Charta were to be disregarded, or that the estates of its subjects were liable to be taken away without trial, without notice and without offense. Even if such authority could be deemed to have been confided by the charter to the general assembly of Rhode Island as an exercise of transcendental sovereignty, before the revolution, it can scarcely be imagined that that great event could have left the people of that State subjected to its unconditioned and arbitrary exercise. The government can scarcely be deemed to be free, where the rights of property are left solely dependent upon the will of a legislative body, without any restraint. The fundamental maxims of a free government seem to require that the rights of personal liberty and private property should be held sacred. At least no court of justice in this country would be warranted in assuming that the power to violate and disregard them—a power so repugnant to the common principles of justice and civil liberty—lurked under any general grant of legislative authority, or ought to be implied from any general expressions of the will of the people. The people ought not to be presumed to part with rights so vital to their security and well-being without very strong and direct expressions of such intention.

"In Terret v. Taylor,[1] it was held, by this court, that a grant or title to lands once made by the legislature, to any person or corporation, is irrevocable, and cannot be reassumed by any subsequent legislative act, and that a dif-

[1] 9 Cranch, 43.

ferent doctrine is utterly inconsistent with the great and fundamental principle of a republican government, and with the rights of the citizens to the free enjoyment of their property lawfully acquired. We know of no case in which a legislative act to transfer the property of A to B, without his consent, has ever been held a constitutional exercise of legislative power in any State in the union. On the contrary, it has been constantly resisted, as inconsistent with just principles, by every judicial tribunal in which it has been attempted to be enforced. We are not prepared, therefore, to admit that the people of Rhode Island had ever delegated to their legislature the power to divest the vested rights of property, and transfer them without the assent of the parties. The counsel for the plaintiffs have themselves admitted that they cannot contend for any such doctrine.

"The question then arises, whether the act of 1792 involves any such exercise of power. It is admitted that the title of an heir by descent, in the real estate of his ancestor, and of a devisee in an estate unconditionally devised to him, is, upon the death of the party under whom he claimed, immediately devolved upon him, and he acquires a vested estate. But this, though true in a general sense, still leaves his title incumbered with all the liens which have been created by the party in his lifetime, or by the law at his decease. It is not an unqualified, though it be a vested interest, and it confers no title, except to what remains after every such lien is discharged. In the present case, the devisee, under the will of Jonathan Jenckes, without doubt, took a vested estate in fee in the lands in Rhode Island. But it was an estate subject to all the qualifications and liens which the laws of that State annexed to those lands. It is not sufficient, to entitle the heirs of the devisee now to recover, to establish the fact that the estate so vested had been divested, but that it had been divested in a manner inconsistent with the principles of law.

"By the laws of Rhode Island, as indeed by the laws of the other New England States (for the same general system pervades them on this subject,) the real estate of testators and intestates stands chargeable with the payment of their debts, upon a deficiency of assets of personal estate. The deficiency being once ascertained in the probate court, a license is granted by the proper judicial tribunal, upon the petition of the executor, or administrator, to sell so much of the real estate as may be necessary to pay the debts and incidental charges. The manner in which the sale is made is prescribed by the general laws. In Massachusetts and Rhode Island, the license to sell is granted, as a matter of course, without notice to the heirs or devisees, upon the mere production of proof from the probate court, of the deficiency of personal assets. And the purchaser at the sale, upon receiving a deed from the executor or administrator, has a complete title, and is in immediately under the deceased, and may enter and recover possession of the estate, notwithstanding any intermediate descents, sales, disseizins, or other transfers of title or seizin. If, therefore, the whole real estate be necessary for the payment of debts, and the whole is sold, the title of the heirs or devisees is, by the general operations of law, divested and superseded; and so, *pro tanto*, in case of a partial sale.

"From this summary statement of the laws of Rhode Island, it is apparent that the devisee, under whom the present plaintiffs claim, took the land in controversy, subject to the lien for the debts of the testator. Her estate was a defeasable estate, liable to be divested upon a sale by the executrix, in the ordinary course of law, for the payment of such debts, and all that she could rightfully claim, would be the residue of the real estate after such debts were fully satisfied. In point of fact, as it appears from the evidence in the case, more debts were due in Rhode Island than the whole value for which all the estate there was sold; and there is nothing to impeach the fairness of the sale. The probate proceedings further show, that the estate was represented to be insolvent; and, in fact, it approached very near to an actual insolvency. So that, upon this posture of the case, if the executrix had proceeded to obtain a license to sell, and had sold the estate according to the general laws of Rhode Island, the devisee and her heirs would have been divested of their whole interest in the estate, in a manner entirely complete and unexceptionable. They have been divested of their formal title in another manner, in favor of creditors entitled to the estate; or, rather, their formal title has been made subservient to the paramount title of the creditors.

"Some suggestions have been thrown out at the bar, intimating a doubt whether the statutes of Rhode Island, giving to its courts authority to sell lands for payment of debts, extended to cases where the deceased was not, at the time of his death, an inhabitant of the State. It is believed that the practical construction of these statutes has been otherwise. But it is unnecessary to consider whether that practical construction be correct or not, inasmuch as the laws of Rhode Island, in all cases, make the real estate of persons deceased chargeable with their debts, whether inhabitants or not. If the authority to enforce such a charge by a sale, be not confided to any subordinate court, it must, if at all, be exercised by the legislature itself. If it be so confided, it still remains to be shown that the legislative is precluded from a concurrent exercise of power.

"What, then, are the objections to the act of 1792? First, it is said that it divests vested rights of property. But it has been already shown that it divests no such rights, except in favor of existing liens, of paramount obligation, and that the estate was vested in the devisee, expressly subject to such rights. Then, again, it is said to be an act of judicial authority, which the legislature was not competent to exercise at all; or, if it could exercise it, it could be only after due notice to all the parties in interest, and a hearing and decree. We do not think that the act is to be considered as a judicial act, but as an exercise of legislation. It purports to be a legislative resolution, and not a decree. As to notice, if it were necessary (and it certainly would be wise and convenient to give notice, where extraordinary efforts of legislation are resorted to, which touch private rights), it might well be presumed, after the lapse of more than thirty years, and the acquiescence of the parties for the same period, that such notice was actually given. But by the general laws of Rhode Island upon this subject, no notice is required to be, or is, in practice, given to heirs or devisees, in cases of sales of this nature; and it would be strange if the legislature might not do, without notice, the same act which it would delegate authority to another to do without notice. If the legislature had authorized a future sale by the executrix for the payment of debts, it is not easy to perceive any sound objection to it. There is nothing in the nature of the act which requires that it should be performed by a judicial tribunal, or that it should be performed by a delegate, instead of the legislature itself. It is remedial in its nature, to give effect to existing rights.

"But it is said that this is a retrospective act, which gives validity to a void transaction. Admitting that it does so, still it does not follow that it may not be within the scope of the legislative authority, in a government like that of Rhode Island, if it does not divest the settled rights of property. A sale had already been made by the executrix under a void authority, but in entire good faith (for it is not attempted to be impeached for fraud), and the proceeds, constituting a fund for the payment of creditors, were ready to be distributed as soon as the sale was made effectual to pass the title. It is but common justice to presume that the legislature was satisfied that the sale was *bona fide*, and for the full value of the estate. No creditors have ever attempted to disturb it. The sale, then, was ratified by the legislature, not to destroy existing rights, but to effectuate them, and in a manner beneficial to the parties. We cannot say that this is an excess of legislative power, unless we are prepared to say that, in a State not having a written constitution, acts of legislation having a retrospective operation, are void as to all persons not assenting thereto, even though they may be for beneficial purposes, and to enforce existing rights. We think that this cannot be assumed, as a general principle, by courts of justice. The present case is not so strong in its circumstances as that of Calder v. Bull,[1] or Rice v. Parkman,[2] in both of which the resolves of the legislature were held to be constitutional."[3]

§ 57. **Confirming Irregular Judicial Proceedings.**— The decision just quoted is extreme in its character, in this, that it affirms the constitutionality of a statute which confirmed proceedings that had, of themselves, not even the shadow of validity. The defect in the title, made good by this statute, did not arise from any irregular exercise of existing authority, but from the palpable absence of all authority whatsoever. The court, under which the executrix had acted, was notoriously without jurisdiction in the matter. In so far as this decision maintains that proceedings, prosecuted without jurisdiction over the person or subject-matter, may be subsequently validated by legislative action, we think it is squarely in conflict with the opinions of the jurists of the present age. But mere irregularities of proceeding, though of so grave a character as to render a judicial or execution sale inoperative, may be deprived of their evil consequences by subsequent legislation. In Pennsylvania, a judgment prematurely entered was confirmed by an act of the legislature, after a sale of the defendant's property had been made under it. "The error in entering the judgment," said the court, " is cured by the confirming

---

[1] 3 Dall. Rep. 386.
[2] 16 Mass. Rep. 326.
[3] Wilkinson v. Leland, 2 Pet. 656.

act; the constitutionality of this, no man can doubt. It impaired no contract, disturbed no vested right, and if ever there was a case in which the legislature ought to stretch forth its strong arm to protect a whole community from an impending evil, caused by mere slips, this was the occasion. Confirming acts are not uncommon—are very useful; deeds acknowledged defectively by *feme coverts* have been confirmed, and proceedings and judgments of commissioned justices of the peace, who were not commissioned agreeably to the constitution, or where their power ceased on the division of the counties, until a new appointment. This law is free from all the odium to which retrospective laws are generally exposed. Where a law is in its nature a contract, where absolute rights are vested under it, a law retrospecting, even if constitutional, would not be extended by any liberal construction, nor would it be construed, by any general words, to embrace cases where actions are brought. Retrospective laws, which only vary the remedies, divest no right, but merely cure a defect in a proceeding otherwise fair—the omission of formalities which do not diminish existing obligations, contrary to their situation when entered into and when prosecuted; for one is consistent with every principle of natural justice, while the other is repugnant. The plaintiff in error could not be injured, whether the judgment was entered on the Monday or Wednesday of the week. It did not deprive him of any opportunity of defense. If he filed a counter statement or plea, appeared and took defense any time in the week, the court would have received it."[1] But, as a general rule, the court will not uphold statutes which interfere with the effect of their pre-existing judgments.[2] In Indiana, however, a

---

[1] Underwood v. Lilly, 10 S. & R. 97.

[2] Hence, the legislature cannot authorize a court to reopen its judgments after the time for appeal has expired. De Chastellux v. Fairchild, 15 Pa. St. 18; s. c., 53 Am. Dec. 570; Hill v. Town of Sunderland, 3 Vt. 507; Davis v. Menasha, 21 Wis. 491; Taylor v. Place, 4 R. I. 324; Lewis

curative act was held valid, which made valid the proceedings of a term of court held without authority of law.¹ But, in this State, the extreme ground is maintained, that a legislature may always make void acts valid, unless restrained by some direct constitutional provision.² In Massachusetts, an executor's sale was confirmed, in a case where she had given no notice, as prescribed by law, of her petition for the license to sell, and the confirmatory act was declared valid. But in this case the heirs had, in writing, assented to the sale.³

§ 58. **Proceedings Based on Void Judgments Cannot be Validated.**—One of the limitations on the enactment of valid curative statutes is, that a legislature cannot make immaterial, by subsequent enactment, an omission which it had no authority to dispense with by previous statute.⁴ It is usually understood that the legislature has no power to authorize an adjudication against a person without giving him any opportunity of making his defense. This he cannot make unless he has some notice of the proceeding against him. There must be something to give the court jurisdiction over his person. If, therefore, the proceedings had in a court are prosecuted without jurisdiction, the legislature cannot subsequently make them valid.⁵ An act was passed by the legislature of Illinois, and being invoked for the purpose of sustaining proceedings where no service of summons had been made on the defendants, its validity was denied in an opinion by Caton, C. J., in the course of which he said: ("If it was competent for the legislature to

v. Webb, 3 Greenl. 326; Denny v. Mattoon, 2 Allen, 379, overruling Braddee v. Brownfield 2 W. & S. 271.

¹ Walpole v. Elliott, 18 Ind. 258.
² Ib.; Andrews v. Russell, 7 Blackf. 474; Grimes v. Doe, 8 Blackf. 371.
³ Sohier v. Mass. Gen'l Hospital, 3 Cush. 483.
⁴ State v. Squires, 26 Ia. 340.
⁵ Hopkins v. Mason, 61 Barb. 469; Hart v. Henderson, 17 Mich. 218; Griffin v. Cunningham, 20 Gratt. 109; Lane v. Nelson, 79 Pa. St. 407; Pryor v. Downey, 50 Cal. 389; s. c., 19 Am. Rep. 656.

make a void proceeding valid, then it has been done in this case. Upon this question we cannot for a moment doubt or hesitate. They can no more impart a binding efficacy to a void proceeding, than they can take one man's property from him and give it to another. Indeed, to do the one is to accomplish the other.] By the decree in this case, the will in question was declared void, and, consequently, if effect be given to the decree, the legacies given to those absent defendants will be taken from them, and given to others, according to our statutes of descents. Until the passage of the act in question, they were not bound by the verdict of the jury in this case, and it could not form the basis of a valid decree. Had the decree been rendered before the passage of the act, it would have been as competent to make that valid, as it was to validate the antecedent proceedings, upon which alone the decree could rest. The want of jurisdiction over the defendants was as fatal to the one as it could be to the other. If we assume the act to be valid, then the legacies, which before belonged to the legatees, have now ceased to be theirs, and this result has been brought about by the legislative act alone. The effect of the act upon them is precisely the same as if it had declared, in direct terms, that the legacies bequeathed by this will to these defendants, should not go to them, but should descend to the heir at law of the testator, according to our law of descent. This, it will not be pretended, they could do directly, and they had no more authority to do it indirectly, by making proceedings binding upon them which were void at law."[1] In the case just cited, no sale had been made. It was a suit in equity to set aside a will. A trial had been had, resulting in favor of the plaintiffs. It was then discovered that certain non-resident minor defendants, who had answered by guardian *ad litem*, had not been properly served with process. The effect sought by the statute

---

[1] McDaniel v. Correll, 19 Ill. 228; s. c., 68 Am. Dec. 587.

was simply to validate a void judgment. In the case of Nelson v. Rountree,[1] it appeared that a judgment had been entered in an action in which the summons was served by publication. There was no authority for such service, because the affidavit for the order of publication failed to show that a cause of action existed against the defendants. The judgment was, therefore, void. The legislature subsequently declared that " all orders of publication, heretofore made, shall be evidence that the court or officer, authorized to grant the same, was satisfied of the existence of all the fact requisite to granting such order or orders, and shall be evidence of the existence of such facts." Perhaps the constitutionality of this statute might have been maintained, on the ground that it simply created a rule of evidence, or shifted the burden of proof from one person to another.[2] The supreme court of the State, however, regarded it as a confirmatory act, and denounced it as follows: " If it was competent for the legislature to make this declaration, then it was competent for it to have declared that to be a judgment, which was before no judgment, and binding on the party against whom formally rendered, when before he was not bound at all; for such is the direct result. It is a proposition, not now to be discussed at this day, that the legislature has no such power."[3] Speaking of an act of assembly purporting to validate certain proceedings in partition, which were void because one of the defendants had no notice of their pendency, the supreme court of Pennsylvania said: " The act itself is unconstitutional and void, as an infringement of the inhibition contained in the ninth section of the declaration of rights, article IX of the constitu-

---

[1] 23 Wis. 367.

[2] The legislature may change the burden of proof by enacting that proceedings theretofore taken in a court of special or limited jurisdiction shall be presumed, *prima facie*, to have been taken rightfully; and thus compel a person assailing such proceedings to show that the court never acquired jurisdiction. Chandler v. Northrop, 24 Barb. 129.

[3] Nelson v. Rountree, 23 Wis. 370.

tion, that no person 'can be deprived of his life, liberty and property, unless by the judgment of his peers, or the law of the land.' What is the act but a mere bold attempt to take the property of A and give it to B? It was not a case in which the mere irregularity of a judgment, or a formal defect in the acknowledgment of a deed, was cured, where the equity of the party is complete, and all that is wanting is legal form. Such were Underwood v. Lilly,[1] Tate v. Stooltzfoos,[2] Satterlee v. Matthewson,[3] and Mercer v. Watson.[4] On the contrary, it is very clearly within the principle of Norman v. Heist,[5] Greenough v. Greenough,[6] De Chastellux v. Fairchild,[7] Bagg's Appeal,[8] Shafer v. Eneu,[9] and Shonk v. Brown.[10] These cases abundantly sustain the position that an act of the legislature cannot take the property of one man and give it to another, and that when it has been attempted to be taken by a judicial proceeding, as a sheriff's sale, which is void for want of jurisdiction, it is not in the power of the legislature to infuse life into that which is dead—to give effect to a mere nullity. That would be essentially a judicial act—to usurp the province of the judiciary—to forestall or reverse their decision.[11] Of course, the legislature can no more validate proceedings before a court or officer incompetent to entertain and decide them, than it can vivify judgments void for want of jurisdiction over the person of the defendant.[12]

[1] 10 S. & R. 97.
[2] 16 S. & R. 35; s. c., 16 Am. Dec. 546.
[3] 16 S. & R. 191.
[4] 1 Watts, 330.
[5] 5 W. & S. 171; s. c., 40 Am. Dec. 496.
[6] 11 Pa. St. 489.
[7] 15 Pa. St. 18; s. c., 53 Am. Dec. 570.
[8] 43 Pa. St. 512.
[9] 54 Pa. St. 304.
[10] 61 Pa. St. 320.
[11] Richards v. Rote, 68 Pa. St. 255.
[12] Denny v. Mattoon 2 Allen, 383; State v. Doherty, 60 Me. 504; Pryor v. Downey, 50 Cal. 389; s. c., 19 Am. Rep. 656.

In Stevens v. Enders,[1] the supreme court of New Jersey determined that, with respect to estates in remainder, the judges of the court of common pleas had no authority to order or approve a sale in partition. In March, 1861, the legislature undertook to validate all sales made in partition, notwithstanding the existence of estates in remainder or reversion, unless the proceedings for partition "shall have been reversed or set aside on *certiorari*, writ of error, or other proceedings to review the same, brought within three years after such partition sale." When this statute came before the court, it was declared unconstitutional on a very forcible opinion, the chief grounds of which were: 1st, that when the partition sale was made, the court had no jurisdiction over either the estate in remainder, or the persons of the remaindermen; 2d, that as a consequence of this want of jurisdiction, the estates in remainder must have, notwithstanding the partition sale, remained vested in the remaindermen, until the passage of the act of March, 1861; 3d, that to allow such estates to be divested by such act, is to take them "without a hearing, or an opportunity for a hearing being given to the owner," and is an infringement upon that part of the bill of rights in the constitution of 1844, declaring that one of the inalienable privileges of men "shall be that of possessing and protecting property." The court also distinguished cases which had arisen under the prior constitution from those existing under the constitution of 1844, showing that, prior to the adoption of the latter constitution, the power of the legislature was, perhaps, as unlimited as that of the legislature of Rhode Island, as established by the decision in Wilkinson v. Leland, but that by the constitution of 1844, the powers of government were distributed into three departments—legislative, executive and judicial—and each department was forbidden from infringing upon the other. "Since

---

[1] 1 Green, 271.

this explicit marking out of the several departments, it has been the general opinion, so far as I can learn, that the legislative power is the only power vested in the legislature. The power of the legislature being then thus limited to this single field of action, how is the enactment of the present law to be vindicated? If it has the effect intended, it takes this vested estate out of these remaindermen and converts it into money. The question whether the owner's land shall, without his assent, be turned into money, has always, at the common law and in this State, been deemed one addressed to the judicial discretion. The right to decide in such junctures has been always confided, in part, to courts of equity."[1]

§ 59. **Defects, other than Jurisdictional, which have been Held Incurable.**—There are other defects, besides jurisdictional ones, on account of which void sales have been pronounced incurable. In Pennsylvania, an execution sale was void because made after the return day of the writ. Subsequently, the legislature enacted that: "All sales of real estate made by sheriffs or coroners, after the return day of their several writs of *levari facias, fieri facias, venditioni exponas*, or other writ of execution, shall not, on account of such irregularity in such proceedings, be set aside, invalidated, or in manner affected; and such sales so made shall be held as good and valid, to all intents and purposes, as if such sale had been made on or before the return day of the writs respectively." The supreme court of the State, in deciding a case arising under this act, asked the questions: "Is this act constitutional? The sale being made contrary to legislative enactment, and declared by this court utterly void, can the legislature validate such a sale to the injury of another party? In plain English, can they take one man's property and give it to another—property which is secured to him by the constitution and laws?" It then answered

---

[1] Maxwell v. Goetschius, 40 N. J. L. 383; s. c., 29 Am. Rep. 242.

the question as follows: "In this case, the purchaser bought in the face of a recent statute which he was bound to know and obey, and purchased with his eyes open. He has no moral claim to have the sale made good. The act of the legislature which covers this case is unconstitutional and void.[1] A sale void on account of fraud practiced by the purchasers cannot be validated by the legislature. It does not come within the principle of that class of cases in which a legislature has been held to have the power to confirm by retroactive laws the acts of public officers, who have exceeded or imperfectly executed their authority."[2]

§ 60. **Informalities may be Waived by Subsequent Curative Acts.**—Where a sale is void for some defect in the proceedings, not jurisdictional in its character, it may, in most States, be validated by subsequent curative act of the legislature.[3] Hence, acts have been adjudged to be constitutional which validated sales which were void because made in violation of the appraisement laws,[4] or based on defective levies or returns,[5] or on charges of unlawful or excessive fees,[6] or made by an officer of another bailiwick from that in which the lands sold were situate.[7] In the opinion of Judge Cooley, "the rule applicable to cases of this description is substantially the following: If the thing wanting, or which failed to be done, and which constitutes the defect in the proceedings, is something, the necessity

---

[1] Dale v. Medcalf, 9 Pa. St. 110. See, also, Orton v. Noonan, 23 Wis. 102.

[2] White M'ts R. R. v. White M'ts R. R., 50 N. H. 56.

[3] Lane v. Nelson, 79 Pa. St. 407; Boyce v. Sinclair, 3 Bush, 261; Beach v. Walker, 6 Conn. 197; Booth v. Booth, 7 Conn. 350; Wildes v. Vanvoorhis, 15 Gray, 139.

[4] Davis v. State Bank, 7 Ind. 316; Thornton v. McGrath, 1 Duv. 349; Boyce v. Sinclair, 3 Bush, 261.

[5] Mather v. Chapman, 6 Conn. 54; Norton v. Pettibone, 7 Conn. 319; s. c., 18 Am. Dec. 116.

[6] Booth v. Booth, 7 Conn. 350.

[7] Menges v. Wertman, 1 Pa. St. 218, overruled; Menges v. Dentler, 33 Pa. St. 495.

for which the legislature might have dispensed with by prior statute, then it is not beyond the power of the legislature to dispense with it by subsequent statute. And if the irregularity consists in doing some act, or in the mode or manner of doing some act, which the legislature might have made immaterial by prior law, it is equally competent to make the same immaterial by a subsequent law."[1] A partition sale was made to a company of persons, but the deed, by their consent, was made to one only, for convenience of selling and conveying. The deed was invalid, because it did not follow the sale and order of confirmation. An act was subsequently passed providing that, on satisfactory proof being made to a court or jury that the lands were fairly sold, in good faith and for a sufficient consideration, the deed should be held valid. This act was held free from constitutional objections.[2] In Massachusetts, an act confirming deeds made by certain executors was held valid, though they "had not previously been appointed and given bond in such a manner as to authorize them to execute the power of sale conferred by the will."[3] But, in this case, the heirs at law of the testator released all their interest in the lands at the time the executor's deed was executed. An extreme case is that of Selsby v. Redlon.[4] Justices' courts were authorized to issue executions at any time within two years after the entry of judgment. Nevertheless, under a misapprehension of the law, the practice

[1] Cooley's Const. Lim. 371. Hence, deeds not executed in the mode prescribed by statute, may be validated by a statute passed subsequent to their execution. Watson v. Mercer, 8 Pet. 88; Chesnut v. Shane's Lessee, 16 Oh. 599; s. c., 47 Am. Dec. 387; Newman v. Samuels, 17 Ia. 528; Shonk v. Brown, 61 Pa. St. 327; Dulany v. Tilghman, 6 G. & J. 461; Journeay v. Gibson, 56 Pa. St. 57; Dentzel v. Waldie, 30 Cal. 138. *Contra*, Pearce v. Patton, 7 B. Mon. 162; s. c., 45 Am. Dec. 61; Russell v. Rumsey, 35 Ill. 362; Ala. L. I. & T. Co. v. Boykin, 38 Ala. 510.
[2] Kearney v. Taylor, 15 How. (U. S.) 494.
[3] Weed v. Donovan, 114 Mass. 183.
[4] 19 Wis. 17.

prevailed, to a considerable extent, of issuing such writs at any time within five years. The legislature passed an act confirming and validating proceedings taken under writs issued more than two years after the entry of judgment. "Was it competent for the legislature, so far as the time of issuing was concerned, to enact that all executions upon judgments of justices of the peace theretofore issued after the expiration of two, but before the lapse of five years from the time the judgments were rendered, should be deemed valid and regular? It seems to me that it was, and that the act operated at once upon all such executions, the invalidity of which had not already been adjudged by some competent court of law or equity. I had occasion to examine the question, and some of the leading authorities upon it, in Hasbrouck v. Milwaukee,[1] and deem it unnecessary to add to what is there said. It appears to me, in the language of Chancellor Kent, to be one of those remedial statutes, not impairing contracts or disturbing absolute vested rights, but going only to confirm rights already existing, and in furtherance of the remedy, by curing defects and adding the means of enforcing existing obligations, the constitutionality of which has always been upheld. The validity of the judgment is not questioned, and the obligation of the debtor to pay not denied. After the execution was issued and the judgment satisfied, the question was whether such satisfaction should stand, and the creditor retain what in justice and equity belonged to him, or whether he should make restoration to his debtor, and be put to a new action to recover his debt. I think an act to relieve debtors in such cases to be not only just and reasonable, but that it is liable to no constitutional objection."[3]

Curative statutes may undoubtedly destroy the force of an objection founded on a mere formality; and, according to many of the authorities, a matter may be regarded

[1] 13 Wis. 50.
[2] Selsby v. Redlon, 19 Wis. 21.

as a mere formality, within the meaning of this rule, if the legislature might, in the first instance, have authorized its omission. Thus, the legislature may unquestionably provide that judgments need not be signed by the judge, or may be entered on a written waiver of service of summons. Hence, it may make valid judgments not so signed,[1] or founded on such waiver of service.[2] It has also been held that a sale, made by a foreign executor, vested with a power of sale by the will, though void when made, because not ordered nor approved by the court, may be validated by subsequent statute, if the right to sell was not dependent on anything but the judgment of the executor, or the sale must therefore have inevitably been ordered and approved, had proper application been made.[3]

§ 61. **Limitation on Effect of Curative Statutes.**—Even in those States where the validity of curative statutes is conceded, their operation is usually limited to the original parties. If a defendant whose property has been so irregularly sold under execution that his title is not divested, sell to a purchaser in good faith, and for value, the title of the latter is regarded as a vested right, which cannot be divested by a subsequent statute. The same rule usually prevails in regard to all legislation enacted for the purpose of confirming deeds which are invalid for some informality. The curative act does not operate against purchasers from the grantor in good faith, and for value, before its passage.[4] The operation of curative acts, has also been denied where the proceedings had been, prior to the passage of the act,

---

[1] Cookerly v. Duncan, 87 Ind. 332.
[2] Muncie Bank v. Miller, 91 Ind. 441.
[3] Smith v. Callighan, 24 N. W. Rep. 50. In Forster v. Forster, 129 Mass. 559, it was decided that a tax sale, void for want of notice of sale, cannot be made valid by statute.
[4] Newman v. Samuels, 17 Ia. 528; Brinton v. Seevers, 12 Ia. 389; Thompson v. Morgan, 6 Minn. 292; Sherwood v. Fleming, 25 Tex. Supp. 408; Wright v. Hawkins, 28 Tex. 452; Menges v. Dentler, 33 Pa. St. 495, overruling Menges v. Wertman, 1 Pa. St. 218.

pronounced void by the judgment of a court of competent jurisdiction;[1] and, in Maine, curative acts do not operate to change the result of suits previously pending.[2]

§ 62. **General Reflections Concerning Curative Statutes.**—It must, we suppose, be conceded that, prior to the adoption of the fourteenth amendment, there was no provision in the constitution of the United States which prohibited the State legislatures from enacting curative statutes validating prior judicial sales and proceedings. The provision of sec. 10, art. 1, forbidding States from passing *ex post facto* laws, applies exclusively to criminal matters and proceedings, and does not inhibit retrospective legislation in civil matters.[3] The same section also provides that no State shall pass any "law impairing the obligation of contracts." The word contracts is sufficiently comprehensive to embrace conveyances. Hence, a State legislature cannot annul or diminish the effect of a valid conveyance.[4] But the federal constitution, while it prohibited the impairing of valid contracts, did not inhibit the validation of void contracts, nor the creation of obligations;[5] nor did it prevent the State legislatures from divesting vested rights in any case where they could do so without impairing the obligation of some pre-existing contract.[6] The fifth amendment to the constitution of the United States declares that "no person shall be deprived of life, liberty or property, without due process of law; nor shall private property be taken for public use without just compensation." The prohibi-

[1] Mayor v. Horn, 26 Md. 194.
[2] Adams v. Palmer, 52 Me. 480.
[3] Story on the Const., secs. 1345, 1398; State v. Squires, 26 Ia. 340; Watson v. Mercer, 8 Pet. 88; Carpenter v. Pennsylvania, 17 How. (U. S.) 456; Calder v. Bull, 3 Dall. 386.
[4] Story on the Const., sec. 1376; Fletcher v. Peck, 6 Cranch, 137; People v. Platt, 17 Johns. 195; Grogan v. San Francisco, 18 Cal. 590; Louisville v. University, 15 B. Mon. 642.
[5] Story on the Const., sec. 1398; Satterlee v. Mathewson, 2 Pet. 380.
[6] Story on the Const., sec. 1398; Satterlee v. Mathewson, 2 Pet. 380; Calder v. Bull, 3 Dall. 386.

tions contained in this amendment are addressed to the federal legislature, and do not operate as limitations of the powers of any of the State legislatures.[1] One of the guarantees contained in the fourteenth amendment is as follows: "Nor shall any State deprive any person of life, liberty or property, without due process of law, nor deny to any person, within its jurisdiction, the equal protection of the laws." This provision, in the language of Chief Justice Waite, speaking for the supreme court of the United States, "adds nothing to the rights of one citizen against another. It simply furnishes an additional guarantee against any encroachment by the States upon the fundamental rights which belong to every citizen as a member of society."[2] But whether this amendment may, in any case, operate as a prohibition against curative laws passed by the States is, perhaps, an immaterial inquiry, for the reason that most, if not all, of the State constitutions, contain limitations which, in substance, withhold the right to deprive any person of his property without due process of law.

Those curative acts which impart validity to judicial or execution sales otherwise void, necessarily result in the transfer of one person's property to another, without the assent of the former. Before the passage of the act, property belonged to A. After its passage, the same property, without any act on the part of A or B, and solely through the operation of the curative statute, is vested in the latter. Such a statute cannot be maintained on the ground that it is a judicial determination, that the title of B is paramount to that of A, for the State constitutions prohibit the legislatures from exercising judicial functions. These constitutions also protect vested rights and prohibit the taking of

---

[1] Barron v. Mayor of Baltimore, 7 Pet. 243; Withers v. Buckley, 20 How. (U. S.) 84.

[2] United States v. Cruikshank, 92 U. S. 542; 3 Cent. L. J. 295; 8 Ch. L. N. 233. See City of Portland v. City of Bangor, 65 Me. 120; 3 Cent. L. J. 651.

property from one person and giving it to another, at least in all cases where there has been no resort to due process of law.¹ But the words "property" and "vested rights," within the meaning of these constitutions, are difficult of definition. They seem not to refer to the legal title merely —not to insure to a man that which at law belongs to him, but which in equity belongs to another. The most justifiable curative legislation is that which does no more than to give a legal sanction to a title which was theretofore good in equity.² So, it is said, legislatures may transmute a moral into a legal obligation;³ and that "a party has no vested right in a defense based upon an informality not affecting his substantial equities;"⁴ that "courts do not regard rights as vested contrary to the justice and equity of the case;"⁵ that "a party cannot have a vested right to do a wrong;"⁶ that "the rules which determine the legislative power in such cases, are broad rules of right and justice."⁷ So, after all, the limitation inserted in the fundamental laws are so construed that their application depends, not on settled principles, but upon notions of right and justice. A man's title may be perfect at law. It may also be unassailable in equity. He has, nevertheless, no vested right in it which he may hold paramount to legislative control, unless, in addition to his perfect title at law and in equity, his title also meets the approval of the judge before whom it is questioned; the latter, in withholding or granting such approval, being governed by certain rules of

---

¹ Cooley's Const. Lim., chap. xi. To ascertain the meaning of "due process of law," and of equivalent terms, see ib.; Kennard v. Louisiana, 8 Ch. L. N. 329; 92 U. S. 480; Walker v. Sauvinet, 3 Cent. L. J. 445; 92 U. S. 90; Murray v. Hoboken L. & I. Co., 18 How. (U. S.) 272; Story on the Const., sec. 1944.

² Chesnut v. Shane, 16 Oh. 599; s. c., 47 Am. Dec. 387.

³ Weister v. Hade, 52 Pa. St. 480.

⁴ Cooley's Const. Lim. 370.

⁵ State v. Newark, 3 Dutch. 197.

⁶ Foster v. Essex Bank, 16 Mass. 245.

⁷ Story on the Const., sec. 1958, by Cooley.

right and justice existing in his own conscience, but not susceptible of that accurate description which would enable us to recognize them in the future, and rely on them for our protection and guidance. Such, at least, seems to be the result of the weight of the authorities.

With respect to curative acts affecting judicial and execution sales, two rules are commonly put forth as tests of their constitutionality. The first is, that what the legislature could have dispensed with before the sale, it may dispense with afterwards;[1] and the second is, that courts do not regard rights as vested contrary to the justice and equity of the case, but will determine the legislative power on broad rules of right and justice. Neither rule has been universally accepted and followed. Thus, though a statute may unquestionably authorize property to be sold for taxes, without the aid of any judicial proceedings whatever, yet where such proceedings were required, and were so prosecuted as to be void for want of jurisdiction over the defendant, it was held that they could not be made valid by subsequent legislation.[2] So, while legislatures may authorize guardians and others to sell property belonging to persons not *sui juris*, without applying to court for authority so to do, yet where such applications are required to be made to some court, and the proceedings of such court are void for want of jurisdiction, they cannot be subsequently made valid.[3] If the rights of one whose property has been sold at a void sale are not to be regarded as vested except when, "upon broad rules of right and justice," they should be so regarded, then the distinction between jurisdictional and other defects is immaterial. For it may be, and frequently is, as unjust to urge a jurisdictional defect, as it is to urge some other irregularity, such, for instance, as the omission to give notice of the sale. In the first case, the

---

[1] Cooley's Const. Lim. 371; Ferguson v. Williams, 58 Ia. 717.
[2] Nelson v. Rountree, 23 Wis. 367.
[3] See sec. 58.

sale may have been fair, a good price realized, and the proceeds applied to pay the debts of the defendant; while, in the second case, the property may have been sacrificed for want of the notice of the sale. If void judicial or execution sales may be made valid, it would seem to be on the ground that the purchaser, by the payment of the money and its application to the benefit of the defendant, obtained an equity which the legislature might recognize and transform into a legal title;[1] that, in such a case, the person whose property was sold has left to him, after the sale and conveyance, a mere technical and unconscionable defense; and that, in such a defense, there can be no vested right. But this view of the question is not invariably correct nor necessarily conclusive. In the first place, everybody is conclusively presumed to be acquainted with the law. It cannot, therefore, be expected that a sale, made in such a manner as to be inoperative under the then existing law, will realize a fair price. Many persons must be deterred from bidding, because they know or suspect that the sale is invalid. He who purchases must be taken to act with his eyes open, and as bidding for a mere chance, rather than for an unquestionable title. All this is equally true, whether the defect be that the judgment is void, or that the sale is invalid from some other vice. He whose property is sacrificed against his will, by being exposed to the hazard of a void sale, has, even in the broad rules of right and justice, rights as sacred as those of the speculating purchaser. The latter is a mere volunteer, risking his money in defiance of the law. He is not imposed on in any manner, nor is there any contract between him and the owner of the property to urge by way of estoppel. But if an execution or judicial sale be void at law, it is usually equally void in equity. The purchaser has no title which is recognized in any prevailing system of law. The judgment debtor is under no obligation which

---

[1] Thornton v. McGrath, 1 Duv. 355.

will warrant any court in compelling him to convey or surrender his property to the purchaser. Why should not those rights which confer a perfect title to property, both at law and in equity, be held to be vested rights? If such rights are not vested, then what additional claim to protection must the owner of property have before his rights become vested? Must he have a moral right or title? and, if so, what does the word moral mean in this connection? Has it some definite signification? or must it, for all the practical purposes of litigation, vary so as to correspond with the moral perceptions of the different judges? In pronouncing the opinion of the supreme court of California, in an action wherein an heir had sued to recover his inheritance, Mr. Justice McKinstry very forcibly said: "As to any vague, indeterminate and indeterminable 'moral equity,' if any such exist, it may well be doubted whether we can recognize such, since the courts have no standard by which to estimate its sufficiency or effectiveness. Even if we could adopt, however, the measure of rights suggested by some of the cases, we are not prepared to hold that the plaintiff in this action may not insist upon his complete legal and equitable title, without violating any principle of morality.[1] Admitting that the estate of the ancestor comes to the heir burdened with the debts of the former, it is still the right of the latter, when courts are organized, or are required by the constitution to be organized, for the settlement of the estates of decedents, to have the debts ascertained and the property applied by a tribunal of competent jurisdiction. And, upon any theory, the doctrine of estoppel, which is claimed to impose an imperfect duty capable of being ripened into a perfect obligation by the legislative will, can have no application, unless a party, by his own contract or other voluntary act, has placed himself in such an attitude that it would be a violation of sound morality

---

[1] 8 Gill, 299.

on his part, for him to adhere to and insist on his legal and equitable rights. It ought not to be made to apply to this plaintiff merely because he was a party, as an infant, to a pretended legal proceeding."[1]

[1] Pryor v. Downey, 50 Cal. 403; s. c., 19 Am. Rep. 656.

CHAPTER VII.

CONSTITUTIONALITY OF SPECIAL STATUTES AUTHORIZING INVOLUNTARY SALES.

SECTION.
63. General Nature of Legislative Sale, and of the Statutes under which they are Made.
64. Of the Power of the Legislature to Provide for the Involuntary Sale of Property.
65. The Constitutionality of Special Laws Authorizing Sale of Property Denied.
66. The Constitutionality of Special Laws Authorizing Sale of Property Sustained.
67. Acts Authorizing Sales by Administrators, Constitutionality Affirmed.
68. On Whom Power of Sale may be Conferred by Special Acts.
69. Of Special Acts Authorizing the Sale of Lands to Pay Debts.
70. Special Act need not Require a Bond for the Application of the Proceeds.
71. Acts Authorizing the Sale of the Lands of Cotenants.
72. Decisions Limiting the Power of Legislatures to Pass Special Laws for the Sale of Property.

§ 63. **General Nature of Legislative Sales and the Special Acts under which they are Made.**—A question very closely allied with judicial sales, is that of involuntary sales made by authority of the legislature, without the assent of the owner of the property, and in the absence of any judicial declaration concerning the necessity or propriety of the sale. Many special statutes have been enacted purporting to confer authority on guardians, administrators, trustees and other persons to sell and convey the estates of their wards, or of minor heirs, or of *cestuis que trust*. Sometimes entire strangers have been appointed as commissioners and invested with powers of sale. Generally, in statutes of this character, the legislature assumes the existence of a state of facts, making a sale either necessary or expedient; and, therefore, empowers some one to make a sale, either according to his discretion, or in the manner and under the circumstances designated in the special statute. Frequently bonds are exacted for the purpose of avoiding the misappropriation of the funds to be realized. Often a report of the sale is required to be made to some judicial tribunal. The functions of this tribunal are usually restricted to inquiring and determining whether the sale has been conducted in conformity with the special act. Whether the sale be required to be *confirmed* by some court or not, it is evident that the authority for selling is purely legislative. This class of sales may, therefore, be styled "legislative sales."

§ 64. **Of the Power of the Legislature to Provide for the Involuntary Sale of Property.**—There can be no question of the authority of the legislature, by general laws, and in proper cases, to authorize the compulsory alienation of real and personal property. The power of the English parliament is absolute. It can regulate the succession to the crown, or alter the established religion of the land. Theoretically, at least, it has uncontrovertible dominion over both persons and property. Hence, it is no cause for wonder that "private acts of parliament" are recognized as among the "assurances by matter of record." In this country, however, the legislature of every State possesses an authority much more restricted than that of parliament. In none of our courts would a statute purporting to take property from one person and vest it in another be treated with any respect. The constitutions of most, and, perhaps, of all of our States, vest the legislative and the judicial functions of government in separate tribunals, and forbid either tribunal from encroaching upon the jurisdiction of the other. Hence, a statute professing to determine the conflicting claims of title, would be as inoperative as a statute directly transferring title from one person to another. But every legislature possesses powers under which it may enforce the collection of debts, provide for the management of the property of persons incapable of caring for themselves, and also for the partition of estates held in cotenancy. The exercise of these powers often involves the compulsory sale of property. Before a debt can be collected by legal compulsion, its existence must be determined. This determination can be made only by some *judicial* authority. Hence, a statute declaring that A is indebted to B, or that the lands of A shall be sold to pay the debts owing from him to B, is unquestionably void, unless the legislature enacting it was competent to exercise judicial functions, or the existence of the debt from A to B is settled by some judicial tribunal. So, if A should die, his heirs would unquestionably succeed to his estate, subject to the right of his creditors to enforce their claims against the estate; and also subject, in case of the minority or other incapacity of the heirs, to the power of the government to make the estate contribute to their education or support. But the existence of debts against A could, during his lifetime, be established only by judicial inquiry. Does this inquiry become any less judicial or any more legislative in its nature by reason of A's death? So, in the event that the minor or other heirs of A are alleged to be in circumstances in which the sale of their estate is either essential to their support, or highly beneficial to their interests, the truth of the allegation ought to be determined in some manner; and this determination, if it does not invariably call for the exercise of judicial functions, can unquestionably be most satisfactorily accomplished through their aid. Hence, the compulsory sale of property is usually governed by general laws, under which the necessity and expediency of the sale are made the subject of judicial inquiry, and the authority to proceed depends upon the judgment or order of some judge or court. Any departure from these general laws is fraught with great danger, and is likely to result in inconsiderate action, if not in unmitigated plunder. Hence, in nearly one-half of the States of this union, constitutional provisions directly inhibit special laws licensing the sale of the lands of minors and other persons under legal disability.[1]

§ 65. **The Constitutionality of Special Laws for the Sale of Property Denied.**—In those States whose constitutions do not directly forbid the enactment of special laws authorizing one person to sell the property of another, such laws have, when drawn in question before the courts, been assailed: 1st, as contravening the spirit of constitutional provisions requiring all laws of a general nature to have a uniform operation; 2d, as in opposition to that provision of the constitution of the United States, which is also incorporated in most of the State constitutions, that no person shall be deprived of life, liberty or property without due process of law;[2] and, 3d, as involving the exercise of judicial functions not possessed by the legislature.

The house of representatives of the State of New Hampshire, in June, 1827, asked the judges of the supreme court of judicature of that State, the following question: "Can the legislature authorize a guardian of minors, by a special act or resolve, to make a valid conveyance of the real estate

---

[1] Cooley's Const. Lim., 3d ed., p. 107, note.
[2] This provision may be found in both the fifth and the fourteenth amendments to the constitution of the United States. As employed in the former, it is a limitation on the powers of the general government only. In the latter amendment, it is designed as a limitation on the powers of the States. Barron v. Mayor of Baltimore, 7 Pet. 243; Withers v. Buckley, 20 How. (U. S.) 84; United States v. Cruikshank, 92 U. S. 542; 3 Cent. L. J. 295; 8 Ch. L. N. 233. See City of Portland v. City of Bangor, 65 Me. 120; 3 Cent. L. J. 651.

of his wards?" The judges answered as follows: "The objection to the exercise of such a power by the legislature is, that it is in its nature both legislative and judicial. It is the province of the legislature to prescribe the rule of law; but to apply it to particular cases is the business of the courts of law. And the thirty-eighth article in the bill of rights declares that, 'in the government of this State, the three essential powers thereof, to-wit: the legislative, executive and judicial, ought to be kept as separate from, and independent of, each other as the nature of a free government will admit, or as is consistent with that chain of connection that binds the whole fabric of the constitution in one indissoluble bond of union and amity.' The exercise of such a power by the legislature can never be necessary. By the existing laws, judges of probate have very extensive jurisdiction to license the sale of the real estate of minors by their guardians. If the jurisdiction of the judges of probate be not sufficiently extensive to reach all proper cases, it may be a good reason why that jurisdiction should be extended, but can hardly be deemed a sufficient reason for the particular interposition of the legislature in an individual case. If there be a defect in the laws they should be amended. Under our institutions all men are viewed as equal, entitled to enjoy equal privileges, and to be governed by equal laws. If it be fit and proper that license should be given to one guardian, under particular circumstances, to sell the estate of his ward, it is fit and proper that all other guardians should, under similar circumstances, have the same license. This is the very genius and spirit of our institutions. And we are of opinion that a particular act of the legislature to authorize the sale of the land of a particular minor, by his guardian, cannot be easily reconciled with the spirit of the article in the bill of rights just cited.

"It is true that the grant of such a license by the legislature to the guardian is intended as a privilege and benefit to the ward. But, by the law of the land, no minor is capable of assenting to a sale of his real estate in such a manner as to bind himself. And no guardian is permitted, by the same law, to determine when the estate of his ward ought and when it ought not to be sold. In the contemplation of the law, the one has not sufficient discretion to judge of the propriety and expediency of the sale of his estate, and the other is not to be intrusted with the power of judging. Such being the general law of the land, it is presumed that the legislature would be unwilling to rest the justification of an act authorizing the sale of a minor's estate upon any assent which the guardian or the minor could give to the proceeding.

"The question, then, is, as it seems to us, can a ward be deprived of his inheritance, without his consent, by an act of the legislature, which is intended to apply to no other individual? The fifteenth article in the bill of rights declares that, no subject shall be deprived of his property 'but by judgment of his peers or the law of the land.' Can an act of the legislature, intended to authorize one man to sell the land of another without his consent, be 'the law of the land,' within the meaning of the constitution? Can it be 'the law of the land' in a free country? If the question proposed to us can be resolved into these questions, as it appears to us it may, we feel entirely confident that the representatives of the people of this State will agree with us in the opinion we feel ourselves bound to express on the question submitted to us: That the legislature cannot authorize the guardian of minors, by a special act or resolve, to make a valid conveyance of the real estate of his wards."[1]

The supreme court of the State of Tennessee, in the year 1836, delivered an opinion in full accord with that of the judges of New Hampshire. In 1825, the legislature of the first named State passed an act authorizing the guardians of certain minors therein specified to sell certain lands in

---

[1] Opinion of the Judges, 4 N. H. 572.

the best manner they could, and declaring that the assets to be produced by such sale should be assets for the payment of the debts of the ancestor of the minors. Under this act a sale was made. Some years afterwards a bill was brought by the minors against the grantee of the purchaser, to recover possession of the lands sold, and also for an accounting for the rents and profits. The legislative sale was adjudged void, because it deprived the minors of their property without due process of law, and because the act purporting to authorize it was a usurpation of the authority of the judiciary.[1]

§ 66. **The Constitutionality of Special Laws Authorizing Sales Sustained.**—Notwithstanding the decisive stand taken by the courts of New Hampshire and Tennessee against special statutes authorizing sales by guardians, such statutes have been sustained in other States so frequently, and in such varying circumstances, that their constitutionality is now almost free from doubt. In 1792, Asaph Rice, by a resolve of the general court of the commonwealth of Massachusetts, was authorized to sell and convey certain real estate, of which he was tenant by courtesy, and of which his children were seized in fee of the remainder expectant on the death of their father. A sale was made by virtue of the authority conferred by this resolve. After the death of the father, the children, by a writ of entry, sought to recover their inheritance. Parker, C. J., delivered the opinion of the court, in the course of which he said: " If the power by which the resolve authorizing the sale in this case was passed were of a judicial nature, it would be very clear that it could not have been exercised by the legislature without violating an express provision of the constitution. But it does not seem to us to be of this description of power; for it was not a case of a controversy between party and party: nor is there any decree or judgment

---

[1] Jones v. Perry, 10 Yerg. 59; s. c., 30 Am. Dec. 430.

affecting the title to property. The only object of the authority granted by the legislature, was to transmute real into personal estate, for purposes beneficial to all who were interested therein. This is a power frequently exercised by the legislature of this State, since the adoption of the constitution, and by the legislatures of the province and of the colony while under the sovereignty of Great Britain, analogous to the power exercised by the British parliament, time out of mind. Indeed, it seems absolutely necessary for the interest of those who, by the general rules of law, are incapacitated from disposing of their property, that a power should exist somewhere to convert lands into money. For, otherwise, minors might suffer, although having property it not being in a condition to yield an income. This power must rest in the legislature of this commonwealth, that body being alone competent to act as the general guardian and protector of those who are disabled to act for themselves. It was undoubtedly wise to delegate the authority to other bodies, whose sessions are regular and constant, and whose structure may enable them more easily to understand the merits of the particular applications brought before him. But it does not follow that, because the power has been delegated by the legislature to courts of law, it is judicial in its character. For aught we see, the same authority might have been given to the selectmen of each town, or to the clerks or registers of the counties, it being a mere ministerial act, certainly requiring discretion, and sometimes knowledge of the law for its due exercise, but still partaking in no degree of the characteristic of judicial power. No one imagines that, under this general authority, the legislature could deprive a citizen of his estate, or impair any valuable contract in which he might be interested. But there seems to be no reason to doubt that, upon his application, or the application of those who properly represent him, if disabled from acting himself, a beneficial change of his estate, or a sale of it for purposes necessary and convenient for the lawful owner, is a just and proper subject for the exercise of that authority. It is, in fact, protecting him in his property, which the legislature is bound to do, and enabling him to derive subsistence, comfort and education from property which might otherwise be wholly useless during that period of life when it might be most beneficially enjoyed." [1] If it be conceded that an infant, lunatic or other person, incompetent to act for himself, is in need of ready money for his sustenance, or for any other pressing necessity, of course the conversion of his estate into money would be authorized by any tribunal having competent authority. Legislative licenses authorizing a sale under such circumstances are generally sustained. [2] Nor is any necessity required to support the exercise of this legislative authority. It seems to be sufficient that the sale is one to which the incompetent person might, if *sui juris*, probably give his assent. Hence, a special statute may be supported if, without any apparent necessity, it sanctions the conversion of real into personal estate. This conversion is presumed to be beneficial to the minor, or, at least, not to be a destruction of his rights of property.[3] Acts have been sustained which authorized guardians to convey lands sold by the ancestor of their wards;[4] or which empowered the guardian of a lunatic to sell the lands of the latter to pay off an incumbrance thereon;[5] or which authorized guardians to convey real estate for the purpose of effecting a compromise with persons

---

[1] Rice v. Parkman, 16 Mass. 329.

[2] Stewart v. Griffith, 33 Mo. 23; Davidson v. Koehler, 76 Ind. 412; Hoyt v. Sprague, 103 U. S. 613.

[3] Carroll v. Olmstead, 16 Oh. 251; Dorsey v. Gilbert, 11 G. & J. 87; Davis v. Helbig, 27 Md. 452; Thurston v. Thurston, 6 R. I. 296; Snowhill v. Snowhill, 3 N. J. Eq. 20; Brenham v. Davidson, 51 Cal. 352; Sohier v. Mass. Gen'l Hospital, 3 Cush. 483; Norris v. Clymer, 2 Pa. St. 281; Clark v. Van Surlay, 15 Wend. 436.

[4] Estep v. Hutchman, 14 S. & R. 435.

[5] Davison v. Johonnot, 7 Met. 388; s. c., 41 Am. Dec. 448.

claiming adversely to the minors.[1] The case last cited determined the constitutionality of an act passed by the legislature of Missouri in the year 1847. This act recited that certain adverse claims existed to a tract of land in the city of St. Louis; that the parties in interest had agreed upon a compromise, to accomplish which mutual deeds of quit-claim were essential; and then the act authorized the guardians of designated minors to execute the conveyances necessary to consummate the compromise. Such a conveyance was executed, and was upheld, though it was subsequently ascertained that the minor's title was valid, and that of the adverse claimants unfounded—the court saying: "It is a question of power, and whilst it is conceded that the legislature has no power to transfer A's property to B, or to authorize anyone else to do so—supposing A and B to be adults and competent to transact their own affairs—the legislature may authorize the guardian, father or mother of a lunatic, infant or idiot, to transfer the estate of the minor, lunatic or idiot. It will be observed that the title of Pelagie, and her daughter Antoinette, was a disputed one. That the claimants under Mackay and Rutgers, really had no valid title, is not important. This was ascertained after the decision of this court, in the case of Norcum v. D'Oench, but it was a matter of conjecture before. The adults had an undoubted right to compromise. If the legislature has power to authorize third persons, guardians, fathers, mothers, etc., to convey the undisputed title of an infant, without regard to insuring the proceeds for the benefit of the infant, why should they be deprived of the right to authorize the compromise of an unsettled claim?"[2]

§ 67. **Acts Authorizing Sales by Administrators; Constitutionality of, Affirmed.**—The cases cited in the preceding section affirmed the constitutionality of laws authorizing sales to be made by the guardians or parents of persons

---

[1] Thomas v. Pullis, 56 Mo. 217.
[2] Ibid.

incapable of acting for themselves. We shall now refer to cases involving the legislative delegation of a like authority to administrators. The weight of the authorities is to the effect that the power may be conferred on an administrator as well as on a parent or guardian.[1] In considering the validity of a sale made under an act of this character, the supreme court of the United States said: "On principle, this process is sustainable. On the death of the ancestor, the land owned by him descends to his heirs. But how do they hold it? They hold it subject to the payment of the debts of the ancestor, in those States where it is liable to such debts. The heirs cannot alien the lands to the prejudice of the creditors. In fact and in law they have no right to the real estate of their ancestors, except that of possession, until the debts shall be paid. As it regards the question of power in the legislature, no objection is perceived to their subjecting the lands of the deceased to the payment of his debts, to the exclusion of his personal property. The legislature regulates descents and the conveyance of real estate. To define the rights of debtor and creditor, is their common duty. The whole range of remedies lies within their province. They may authorize a guardian to convey the lands of an infant; and, indeed, they may give capacity to the infant himself to convey them.' The idea that the lands of an infant which have descended to him, cannot be made responsible for the payment of the debts of the ancestor, except through a decree of a court of chancery, is novel and unfounded. So far from this being the case, no doubt is entertained that the legislature of a State have the power to subject the lands of a deceased person to execution in the same manner as if

[1] Doe v. Douglas, 8 Blackf. 10; s. c., 44 Am. Dec. 732; Kibby v. Chitwood, 4 Mon. 91; s. c., 16 Am. Dec. 143; Williamson v. Williamson, 3 S. & M. 715, 745; s. c., 41 Am. Dec. 636; Gannett v. Leonard, 47 Mo. 205; Holman's Heirs v. Bank of Norfolk, 12 Ala. 369, 415; Herbert v. Herbert, Breese, 354; s. c., 12 Am. Dec. 192; Todd v. Flournoy, 56 Ala. 99; Watson v. Oates, 58 Ala. 647; Tindal v. Drake, 60 Ala. 170.

he were living. The mode in which this shall be done is a question of policy, and rests in the discretion of the legislature. The law under which the lot in dispute was sold, decides no fact binding on creditors or heirs. If the administratrix and Brown have acted fraudulently in procuring the passage of this act, or in the sale under it, relief may be given on that ground. But the act does nothing more than provide a remedy, which is strictly within the power of the legislature."[1]

§ 68. **On Whom Power of Sale may be Conferred by Special Acts.**—It does not appear to be necessary that the person authorized by a special act of the legislature to sell the property of another should be an administrator or guardian by regular appointment of the courts of the State where the sale is to be made, nor, indeed, that he should have any official character whatever, nor that he should be a relative of the person for whom he is authorized to act. His authority rests on the special act, and not on his other relations with the incompetent person. The legislature of the State, wherein the land lies, may authorize its sale and conveyance by an administrator residing and appointed in another State or by her attorneys.[2] In Kentucky, an act was sustained which, after reciting that no one would administer of the estate of a deceased person, appointed three commissioners with power to sell so much of such estate as would be necessary to pay his debts.[3] An act of the legislature of California, approved May 6, 1861, purported to authorize Mary Ann Paty Daley, the mother and guardian of Francis William Paty, a minor, to sell any or all of his real estate. In November, prior to the passage of this act, Mrs. Daley had been appointed guardian of her son by the probate judge of Plymouth county, in the State of Massa-

---

[1] Watkins v. Holman, 16 Pet. 62.
[2] Holman's Heirs v. Bank of Norfolk, 12 Ala. 369, 415; Watkins v. Holman, 16 Pet. 25; Boon v. Bowers, 30 Miss. 246.
[3] Shehan's Heirs v. Barnett's Heirs, 6 Mon. 593.

chusetts. In May, 1856, she received a like appointment from the chief justice of the Hawaiian Islands. She was never appointed guardian in California. She made sales and conveyances under this act. These sales were declared void, not on the ground that the statute was unconstitutional, but because she had never been appointed guardian in California. "The statute," said the court, "does not purport, in any part of it, to nominate Martha Ann Paty Daley guardian of the infant; it simply assumes that she is, or—when the sale shall be made—will be guardian of his estate; exercising the ordinary functions, and charged with the ordinary responsibilities of guardians. The power was given to her in her capacity as guardian, and not as an individual; as she failed to secure an appointment as guardian, the attempted sale was void."[1] Frequently property is vested in trustees for the benefit of persons incapable of acting for themselves. When this is the case, the legislature may authorize sales and conveyances to the same extent as when property is in the hands of administrators or guardians. In 1802, Mary Clark devised certain lands to Benjamin Moore, and two other persons, in trust: 1st, to receive the rents, issues and profits thereof, and pay the same to Thomas B. Clarke during his life; 2d, after the death of Thomas B. Clarke, to convey the premises to his lawful issue in fee; 3d, if he should not have lawful issue, then to convey the premises to Clement C. Moore. In 1814, the legislature, upon the petition of Thomas B. Clarke, and with the concurrence of the trustees named in the will, and of Moore, the contingent remainderman, passed an act authorizing the sale of a portion of the real estate for the purpose of *creating an income* for the benefit and support of Thomas B. Clarke, his family and children; the principal, after his death, to be paid according to the trusts in the will of Mary Clarke. In 1815, a further act was passed

[1] Paty v. Smith, 50 Cal. 159; McNeil v. First Cong. Society, 4 W. C. Rep. 424.

reciting that Moore, the contingent remainderman, had conveyed his interest to Thomas B. Clarke, and " authorizing Clarke to do and perform every act in relation to the property, which the act of 1814 had directed might be performed by trustees to be appointed by the chancellor; but no sale was to be made by Clarke until he procured the assent of the chancellor; and when a sale was made, the proceeds were to be invested, and an annual account of the *principal* rendered, but the *interest* Clarke was authorized to apply to *his own use and benefit, and for the maintenance and education of his children.*" Sales were made under these acts. The constitutionality of these acts was discussed in the highest courts of the State and of the nation, and was always sustained. It was held: 1st, that it was competent for the legislature to change the trustees appointed by the will of Mrs. Clarke, and to vest their powers in Thomas B. Clarke; 2d, that it was equally within the power of the legislature to provide for the sale of the interest of the children of Clarke, in order that they might at once have the benefit of the estate for their better support and education during the most helpless period of their lives.[1] The litigation arising under the will of Mrs. Clarke and these special acts of the legislature was carried on, in various courts and forms, during nearly half a century; and has occasioned the most exhaustive discussions, both of the power of the legislatures, by special acts, to authorize the sale of the property of persons incapable of acting for themselves, and of the nature and effect of such sales when conducted under the supervision of judicial authority.[2] The power which is competent

---

[1] Clarke v. Van Surlay, 15 Wend. 436; Leggett v. Hunter, 19 N. Y. 445.
[2] Clarke v. Van Surlay, 15 Wend. 436; Sinclair v. Jackson, 8 Cowen, 543; Cochran v. Van Surlay, 20 Wend. 365; s. c., 32 Am. Dec. 570; Williamson v. Berry, 8 How. (U. S.) 495; Towle v. Forney, 14 N. Y. 423; Williamson v. I. P. Congregation, 8 How. (U. S.) 565; Suydam v. Williamson, 24 How. (U. S.) 427; Williamson v. Ball, 8 How. (U. S.) 566; Williamson v. Suydam, 6 Wall. 723.

to change trustees and provide for the sale of property in which infants are interested, can deal with like efficiency with property given for the purposes of charity;[1] or which is vested in trustees, or other persons, for the benefit of persons not *in esse*.[2]

In the case of Lincoln v. Alexander,[3] the defendants sought to maintain their right to the possession of real property which had been distributed to plaintiffs by the probate court, by proving a sale to them by the plaintiff's mother, acting under the authority of a special statute directing her to make such sale, and to retain and use the proceeds for the maintenance of plaintiffs who were then minors. It appeared that, prior to the enactment of such statute, the stepfather of the minors had been appointed their guardian, and had assumed the management and taken possession of their estates. The plaintiffs recovered chiefly, we presume, on the ground that while there is a guardian fully competent to act, the legislature cannot, by special statute, divest him of his powers, or some portion thereof, and confer them on some other person, though there are intimations in the opinion that the sale of the property of minors cannot be authorized, in the absence of special circumstances, not here shown to exist. The court said: "In Brenham v. Davidson,[4] the statute which was under review in that case, conferred the power of sale on the guardian of the minor, and the sale was to be approved by the probate court. The proceeds of the sale were to be reinvested for the benefit of the minor; and, moreover, no sale was to be made unless the mother of the minor, who held an undivided interest in the property, united in the sale and conveyance. Under these circumstances, we held that the case was one not provided for by the general law,

---

[1] Matter of Trustees N. Y. P. E. Pub. School, 31 N. Y. 592.
[2] Matter of Bull, 45 Barb. 334; Leggett v. Hunter, 19 N. Y. 445.
[3] 52 Cal. 485; s. c., 28 Am. Rep. 639.
[4] 51 Cal. 352.

to authorize the real estate of the minor to be converted into money by the guardian, if the probate court approves the sale. But, in the case at bar, the minors had a duly qualified and acting statutory guardian at the time of the passage of the special act, and the general law provided an appropriate method by which the probate court could order a sale of the real estate of the minors by the guardian, if a sale was necessary for their education and support. The special act conferred the power of sale, not upon the guardian, but upon the mother of the minors, who was not their guardian, and had no interest in the property. Nor were any conditions imposed upon her, except that she should first execute a bond, to be approved by the probate judge, conditioned that the proceeds of the sale should be appropriated to the support and education of the minors; and that the sale should not be valid unless confirmed by the probate court previous to the execution of the deed. In treating of the rights and powers of statutory guardians of the estate of minors, Mr. Schouler, in his treatise on Domestic Relations (p. 471), says: 'The recognized principle is, that such guardians have an authority coupled with an interest, not a bare authority;' and such we understand to be the well settled rule. The statute under consideration, attempts to take the estate of the minors out of the hands of their guardian, and to withdraw it from the control of the probate court, which, under the general law, had ample authority to order it be sold, and the proceeds to be applied to the support and education of the minors. It wholly ignores the rights and powers of the guardian, who had an authority *coupled with an interest;* withdraws the estate from the jurisdiction and control of the probate court, which that court might rightfully exercise under the general law; and attempts to substitute another person for the guardian, with authority to dispose of the estate absolutely, on no other condition than those already mentioned. No adjudicated case has been called to our attention, in which the exercise of such a power by the legislature has been upheld. In his work on Constitutional Limitations, at page 98, Judge Cooley, in discussing legislation of this character, says: 'The rule upon this subject, as we deduce it from the authorities, seems to be this: If the party *standing in the position of trustee*, applies for permission to make the sale, for a purpose apparently for the interest of the *cestui que trust*, and there are no adverse interests to be considered and adjudicated, the case is not one which requires judicial action; but it is optional with the legislature to grant the writ by statute, or to refer the case to the courts for consideration, according as the one course or the other, or considerations of policy, may seem desirable.' But, in the present case, it does not appear that the application was made by a party 'standing in the position of trustee,' and there were 'adverse interests to be considered and adjudicated,' to-wit: those of the guardian. Upon the face of the act there is nothing to show that the legislature was informed that a general guardian of the estates of these infants had actually been appointed. It is fairly to be presumed that they were ignorant of that fact. At all events, in view of the facts now found by the court below, the act cannot be permitted to operate, since, under the circumstances, it would be judicial and not legislative in its character, and for that reason unconstitutional."

§ 69. **Of Special Acts Authorizing the Sale of Lands to Pay Debts.**—As the estate of an ancestor descends to his heirs, subject to the right of the creditors of the former to compel such estate to contribute to the payment of their claims, a special act to authorize the sale of property for the payment of such claims seems to be one of the most defensible acts of special legislation; and so it is, if the validity and existence of the claims be conceded. But special acts to raise funds for the payment of debts have been more persistently and plausibly assailed than acts for any other purpose short of ostensible confiscation. If such an act is so expressed as to preclude the parties in interest from disputing the validity of the debts, it is unquestionably void, because it is a usurpation of judicial authority. In 1827, the legislature of Illinois, by a special act, authorized John Lane to sell so much of the lands of the late Christopher Robinson, deceased, as should prove sufficient to raise the sum of $1,008.87, and interest and cost of sale. The proceeds of the sale were to be applied to the extinguishment of the claims of said Lane and one John Brown for moneys advanced and liabilities incurred on account of Robinson's estate. This act was held to be clearly beyond the authority of the legislature, because the existence of the indebtedness from Robinson's estate to Brown and Lane, and the consequent right of Brown and Lane to satisfaction out of the proceeds of the estate, could only be ascertained as the result of a judicial investigation, which the legislature was incompetent to conduct. The act was also thought to contravene the constitutional provision, that " no freeman shall be disseized of his freehold, but by the judgment of his peers, or the law of the land." [1] The supreme court of Illinois has now taken a position far in advance of that assumed in the case just cited, and will not tolerate any special legislation authorizing the conveyance of real estate to pay debts, unless such debts have first been judicially established. In 1823, the legislature of that State authorized John Rice Jones, administrator of Thomas Brady, deceased, to sell and convey lands, the proceeds to be assets in the hands of the administrator, to be appropriated to the payment of the debts of the deceased, and the balance, if any, to be distributed between his children. Of this act, and a sale made by its authority, the court said: " When the act in question was passed, and when the land was sold, the title was in the heirs of Brady, subject to be divested, if necessary, for the payment of his debts. But

---

[1] Lane v. Dorman, 3 Scam. 238; s. c., 36 Am. Dec. 543; followed in Dubois v. McLean, 4 McLean, 486.

the legislature had no more right or power to assume that he died owing debts, and, on that assumption, to authorize his administrator to sell lands vested in his heirs for the purpose of holding the proceeds as assets, without any judicial inquiry as to the existence of such debts before executing the power, than it would have had, in his lifetime, the right or power to authorize the sheriff of the county where he lived to sell his land, and hold the proceeds for the payment of whatever debts he might owe." [1] The conclusion here announced is one which, upon principle, meets our full concurrence. But we understand the decided preponderance of the authorities to be in favor of sustaining special acts authorizing sales for the payment of the debts of the deceased owner of property, even in advance of the judicial ascertainment of such debts, provided the act leaves the existence of such debts open to inquiry.[2]

§ 70. **Special Act need not Require a Bond for the Application of the Proceeds.**—Special acts, authorizing the sale by one person of the property of another, generally contain precautionary provisions tending to secure the honest exercise of the authority conferred. Bonds are usually exacted, conditioned for the proper appropriation of the proceeds of the sale. By this means, the interests of heirs and creditors are exempted from needless peril. These precautions seem not to be essential to the validity of the act. The question is one of power. The existence of the power being established, the propriety of its exercise rests solely with the legislature. If, through misplaced confidence or reckless inattention to the duties of its trust, the legislature confers the power of sale on a person who, being

---

[1] Rozier v. Fagan, 46 Ill. 405; Davenport v. Young, 16 Ill. 548; s. c., 63 Am. Dec. 320.

[2] Watkins v. Holman, 16 Pet. 25; Davison v. Johonnot, 7 Met. 388; s. c., 41 Am. Dec. 448; Shehan's Heirs v. Barnett's Heirs, 6 Mon. 593; Holman's Heirs v. Bank of Norfolk. 12 Ala. 369; Kibby v. Chitwood, 4 Mon. 91; s. c., 16 Am. Dec. 143; Williamson v. Williamson, 3 S. & M. 715, 745; s. c., 41 Am. Dec. 636.

required to furnish no security, squanders the proceeds of the sale, and thus defrauds the heirs of their inheritance and the creditors of their means of enforcing payment, the sale is not, on that account, invalid.[1]

§ 71. **Acts for the Sale of Lands of Co-Tenants.**—The power of the legislature to authorize, by general laws, the sale of the lands of co-tenants for the purposes of partition, where the necessity of the sale is judicially determined, is unquestionable.[2] So there is little or no doubt of the constitutionality of a special act authorizing a co-tenant to petition a court of competent jurisdiction for the sale of the lands of a co-tenancy, and also authorizing the court, upon being satisfied that a division of the property among the co-tenants is extremely difficult, if not impracticable, to order a sale of the premises and a division of the proceeds among the parties in interest.[3] Such an act leaves the necessity and expediency of the sale to be determined by the judiciary. Special acts which do this are free from constitutional objections, except in those States whose constitutions forbid special legislation.[4] In Pennsylvania, an act was sustained which empowered one of several heirs, without the aid of any judicial proceedings, to sell the lands descended from their common ancestor, and divide the proceeds among the co-heirs;[5] and a decision similar in spirit has been made in Massachusetts.[6]

§ 72. **Decisions Limiting the Power of Legislatures to Pass Special Laws for the Sale of Property.**—We shall now call attention to decisions which, though pronounced by courts which concede the power of a legislature to pass special acts authorizing the sale of property, prescribe

---

[1] Gannett v. Leonard, 47 Mo. 205; Thomas v. Pullis, 56 Mo. 218.
[2] Freeman on Cotenancy and Partition, 540.
[3] Edwards v. Pope, 3 Scam. 465.
[4] Florentine v. Barton, 2 Wall. 210.
[5] Fullerton v. McArthur, 1 Grant's Ca. 232.
[6] Soheir v. Mass. Gen'l Hospital, 3 Cush. 483.

limits beyond which the power is not recognized. In 1831, Thomas Poole devised his real estate to his executors in trust: 1st, to permit his daughter, Eliza, to occupy the same, and take the rents and profits thereof during her natural life; 2d, upon her death, the lands were to vest in her lawful issue, and, in default of such issue, then in all the testator's surviving grandchildren. By special acts, passed in 1837 and 1849, the executors were authorized to sell and convey the real estate, and, with the proceeds, to pay all charges and assessments against the lands, and also the costs of sales and commissions. The surplus was then to be disposed of in the manner specified in the will for the disposition of the real estate. A sale was made under these acts. A case was then agreed upon and submitted, for the purpose of ascertaining whether the purchaser could acquire a valid title. It appeared that the daughter, Eliza, was still living, and that she had two children. The act was held unconstitutional, upon grounds which are not stated in the opinion of the court, with sufficient clearness to enable us to feel confident that we correctly understand them. We judge, however, that the reasoning controlling the decision of the court was substantially this: No necessity existed for the sale; there were no charges, liens or assessments against the property; and no infancy or other necessity shown as to the parties interested under the will; and that, under these circumstances, the acts authorized the taking of property from one person and transferring it to another without any reason.[1] Whether the children of Eliza, "who had a vested remainder in fee, in the premises in question, as tenants in common, subject to open and let in after-born issue of their mother, as tenants in common with them, and liable, however, to be divested by their deaths during the lifetime of their mother," were minors or adults, the report of the case very singularly omits to mention. The

[1] Powers v. Bergen, 6 N. Y. 358. See Leggett v. Hunter, 19 N. Y. 445.

following reasoning of the court, in this case, tends very strongly toward the overthrow of all legislation authorizing the transfer of the property of one person by another, without any imperative necessity, and without the assent of the owner: "If the power exists to take the property of one, without his consent, and transfer it to another, it may as well be exercised without making any compensation as with it; for there is no provision in the constitution that just compensation shall be made to the owner when his property shall be taken for *private* use. The power of making contracts, for the sale and disposition of private property for individual owners, has not been delegated to the legislature or to others, through or by any agency conferred on them for such purpose by the legislature; and if the title of A to property can, without his fault or consent, be transferred to B, it may as well be effected without as with consideration."[1]

In California, it is settled that the legislature cannot authorize an administrator to sell, at his discretion, the lands of his intestate, as in his judgment will best promote the interest of those entitled to the estate. In this case, the heirs of the deceased consisted of his widow and minor children. We make the following quotations from the opinion of the court: "It is undoubtedly within the scope of legislative authority to direct that the debts be paid from the realty instead of the personal property; or, as is done in some States, that the heir need not be made a party to the proceeding to obtain a sale of the real estate, or that the administrator may sell without any order of the court whatever. But all these acts must be for the satisfaction of these liens, which are held to be paramount to the claims of the heirs or devisees.

"Laws which prescribe the manner in which these paramount claims shall be satisfied, are held to be entirely

---

[1] Powers v. Bergen, 6 N. Y. 367.

remedial; and it is upon this ground that the courts have upheld acts authorizing the administrator to sell at private sale, or in some mode not provided in the general law, the land of a deceased person. Such acts have been uniformly held valid where it appeared to be in execution of these liens, and the act was not liable to the objection that, in passing it, the legislature usurped judicial functions; as, for instance, in directing a sale to pay a particular debt, thereby ascertaining the existence of a debt by legislative enactment.

" In all the cases to which our attention has been called by the plaintiff, the decision was put upon this ground. The duty of an administrator is to take charge of the estate for the purpose of settling the claims, and when they have been satisfied, it is his duty to pass it over to the heir, whose absolute property it then becomes. To allow the administrator to sell, to promote the interest of those entitled to the estate, would be to pass beyond the functions of an administrator, and constitute him the forced agent of the living for the management of their estates.

" In this case it does not appear, from the proceedings in the probate court upon the sale, that there were any debts of the deceased at the time of the sale, nor does it appear that the sale was to raise money for the support of the family, or to pay the expenses of administration. The special act does not purport to authorize a sale for the payment of the debts, allowances to the family, or expenses of administration. On the contrary, it expressly authorizes a sale, for the purpose of speculating in the interest of the owners of the property—that is, the heirs. It provides that the administrator may sell, at his discretion, ' the whole or any part of the real estate, or any right, title or interest therein claimed, held or owned by the said Charles White, at the time of his death, as in the judgment of the administrator will best promote the interest of those entitled to the estate.' The probate judge may confirm or set aside the sale, as he may deem just and proper, and for the best interests of the estate.

"Upon the death of the ancestor the heir becomes vested at once with the full property, subject to the liens we have mentioned; and, subject to these liens, and the temporary right of possession of the administrator, he may at once sell and dispose of the property, and has the same right to judge for himself of the relative advantages of selling or holding that any other owner has. His estate is indefeasible, except in satisfaction of these prior liens, and the legislature has no more right to order a sale of his vested interest in his inheritance, because it will be, in the estimation of the administrator and the probate judge, for his advantage, than it has to direct the sale of the property of any other person acquired in any other way. * * It is not contended that the legislature has the power to direct the sale and conveyance of private property for other than public uses. This question was fully considered, however, by us in Sherman v. Buick,[1] and decided in the negative, and that conclusion is fully sustained by the numerous authorities cited by the defendant."[2]

We are unable to concur with the supreme court of California in the opinion foreshadowed in Brenham v. Story, and adopted in Brenham v. Davidson,[3] that the power of the legislature to confer authority on guardians is, where the persons in interest are not *sui juris*, any more ample than its power to confer like authority in a like case on administrators. If the legislature has the power to authorize sales, we cannot conceive that it is limited in the choice of agents to execute the power. It is true that the duties of administrators and guardians are somewhat different under the general laws in force in most of the States. But when a special act is passed, the power to be exercised is

---

[1] 32 Cal. 241.
[2] Brenham v. Story, 39 Cal. 185.
[3] Brenham v. Davidson, 51 Cal. 352.

delegated and prescribed by the special act, and not by the general law. The power of the agent is not, therefore, limited by the fact that, before the passage of the act, he was an administrator, and, as such, had no authority, under the general law, to make a sale when, in his discretion, he thought best. Special acts authorizing sales are maintainable, if at all, because, in the language of Chancellor Walworth, "It is within the power of the legislature, as *parens patriæ*, to prescribe such rules and regulations as it may deem proper for the superintendence, disposition and management of the property and effects of infants, lunatics and other persons who are incapable of managing their own affairs."[1] If the persons interested in an estate are thus incapable, we see no reason why the power of disposing of their estate may not be delegated to an administrator, or even to a stranger, as well as to the guardian. The two California cases last cited are, therefore, irreconcilable in principle, and one or the other ought to be overruled; for, in each case, the legislature authorized a sale to be made without the assent of the owner of the property, and in the absence of any disclosed necessity therefor. In each case the person designated by the legislature was invested with a discretion to make the sale as he might deem best, except that, in the one case, he was instructed to promote the interest of those interested in the estate, while in the other, no such instruction was given. And yet the latter was upheld and the former suffered to fall, and this upon the ground that in the one case the person selected by the special act was a guardian, and in the other, he was an administrator.[2] In the case of a guardian's sale, the persons whose property is to be sold are within the reason of the rule, as stated by Chancellor Walworth. In the case of a sale by an administrator, the heirs may or may not be within the reason of

---

[1] Cochran v. Van Surlay, 20 Wend. 373; s. c., 32 Am. Dec. 570.
[2] See Brenham v. Davidson, 51 Cal. 352; Brenham v. Story, 39 Cal. 185.

the rule as thus stated. If all the owners of the property are not *sui juris*, and are, therefore, within the reason of the rule, then the sale should be sustained, whether the agent selected by the legislature be an administrator or a guardian, or have no other official capacity than that given him by the act. If, on the other hand, any of the owners be *sui juris*, the sale must fall, if made against his will, whether the agent appointed to make it is a guardian or an administrator. Persons regarded in law as capable of conducting their own affairs, are entitled to act for themselves. They are the sole judges of the advisability of selling their property. The legislature cannot, against *their* will, empower any other person to sell and convey *their* interests, even though infants, or persons not *in esse* have estates and interests in the same parcels of property.[1]

[1] Brevoort v. Grace, 53 N. Y. 245; Shoenberger v. School Directors, 32 Pa. St. 34.

INDEX.

N. B.—The figures refer to the section numbers.

A.

ACQUIESCENCE,
    estoppel arising from, 43.

ADMINISTRATION,
    grant of, when void, 2.
    on estate of living person, 4.

ADMINISTRATOR,
    with will annexed, cannot exercise discretionary power, 9.
    acting also as guardian, 17.
    sale to, or to attorney of, 33.

ADMINISTRATORS AND EXECUTORS,
    if appointment of, is void, a sale by, is equally so, 2, 10.
    new, cannot be appointed without removing old, 7.
    validity of acts of administrator, how affected by subsequent probate of will, 4.
    when may make sales without leave of court, 9.
    must qualify before acting, 10.
    purchase by, at their own sales, 33.
    purchase by attorney of, 33.
    authority of, is limited to state where appointed, 10.
    sale by foreign, 10.
    conveyances by, 46.
    conveyances by, when void because not in proper form, 47.
    conveyances by, when compelled or reformed in equity, 55.
    constitutionality of acts ratifying sales by, 56-62.
    constitutionality of special acts authorizing sales by, without order of court, 63-72.

ADVERSE POSSESSION.
    does not make judicial or execution sale of realty void, 38.

APPRAISEMENT,
    sale without, whether void, 27.

AUCTION,
> failure to sell at, 32.
> sale at, when no by-standers are present, 32.

B.

BID,
> when and by whom may be made, 32.
> non-payment of, 41.
> release from, because of defects in the proceedings, 48.
> release from, because of defects in the title, 48.
> resisting payment of, 48.

BOND,
> failure to give, held fatal to probate sale, 22.

C.

CLASSIFICATION,
> of void sales, 1.

COLLATERAL ATTACKS,
> on jurisdiction of probate courts, 4, 8.
> on jurisdiction of courts generally, 8.
> none allowed, to show error or fraud in granting order of sale, 14, 20.

COLLUSION,
> whether presumed because no third persons were present at the sale, 32.

CONFIRMATION OF SALE,
> notice of motion for, 42.
> necessity of, 43.
> conveyance without, is void, 43.
> presumption of, 43.
> ratification of sales never confirmed by court, 43.
> precludes future objections by purchasers to title, 48.
> failure of clerk to enter order of, 43.
> effect of, as an adjudication, 44.
> what irregularities are waived by, 44.
> does not validate void sales, 44.
> may be made to a person substituted in place of original bidder, 44.
> by subsequent legislation, 56, 62.

CONSTITUTION OF UNITED STATES,
> prohibition of *ex post facto* laws, 62.
> prohibition of laws impairing obligations of contracts, 62.
> protection of vested rights, and of life, liberty and property, 62.

CONSTITUTIONALITY,
    of laws taking property from one person and giving it to another, 56.
    of laws revoking and annulling prior grants, 56.
    of laws confirming judgments irregularly entered, 57.
    of laws confirming void judgments, 58.
    of laws confirming sales void for informalities, 59, 60.
    of laws confirming sales void for fraud, 60.
    of general laws authorizing compulsory sales, 64.
    of special laws authorizing involuntary sales denied, 65.
    of special laws authorizing involuntary sales sustained, 66, 67.
    of special laws authorizing sale by person not a guardian, 68.
    of special laws authorizing sale of property to pay debts, 69.
    of special laws authorizing sale of property of co-tenants, 71.
    of special laws authorizing sale of property, limitations on, 72.

CONVEYANCES,
    are essential to transfer of legal title, 45.
    within what time may be made, 46.
    made before payment of purchase money, 46.
    to persons not authorized to receive, are void, 46.
    when void because not in proper form, 47.
    mistaken recitals do not make void, 47.
    compelling, in equity, 55.
    reforming, in equity, 55.
    special statutes authorizing, 66.

COUNTY,
    division of, what officer may sell after, 29.

CURATIVE STATUTES,
    validity of, under constitution of United States, 56, 62.
    with reference to irregular judicial proceedings, 57.
    with reference to void judicial proceedings, 58.
    with reference to various informalities and defects, 59, 60.
    with reference to sales void for fraud, 59.
    limitations on operation of, 61.

D.

DEFINITIONS,
    of execution sale, 1.
    of judicial sale, 1.
    of jurisdiction, 1.
    of legislative sales, 63.
    of vested rights, 61.

DESCRIPTION,
    in judgment and deed cannot be reformed, 55.
    in order of sale, 11, 20.

DISQUALIFIED JUDGE,
acts of, when void, 6.

E.

EQUITY,
when will subrogate purchaser to claims discharged through his purchase, 51-53.
when will give purchaser lien for his purchase money, 52, 53.
cannot aid defective execution of statutory powers, 55.
cannot correct mistakes in execution of statutory powers, 55.
may compel the execution of a proper conveyance, 55.
may sometimes reform conveyances made by sheriffs, administrators, etc., 55.

EQUITY SALES,
caveat emptor, whether the rule of, 48.

ESTOPPEL,
against avoiding sales, 50.

EXECUTION SALES,
defined, 1.
irregularities in, are not ordinarily fatal, 21.
without issue of any writ, are void, 23.
must be supported by a valid writ, 23.
under writ issued on satisfied judgment, 23, note.
under writ issued at an improper time, 24.
under writ issued after death of a party, 24.
under writ issued after abolition of the court, 23, note.
under writ issued before judgment is rendered, 24.
under writ issued on transcript of justice's judgment, 24.
under writ insufficient in form, 25.
variances not fatal to, 25.
without levy, 26.
without inquisition or appraisement, 27.
whether void for want of notice, 28.
by whom may be made, 29.
when may be made, 30.
where may be made, 31.
must be at auction, 32.
where there are no by-standers, 32.
to or for officer conducting the sale, 33.
for too great an amount, 34.
of property not subject to sale, is void, 35.
of property of a stranger to the writ, is void, 35.
of property in adverse possession, 38.

EXECUTION SALES—Continued.
    made *en masse*, whether void, 39.
    effect of fraudulent devices, 40, 41.
    confirmation of, 43.
    rights of purchaser, when sale is void, 51, 52.
    curing defects in, by subsequent legislation, 56-62.
EXECUTION, WRITS OF,
    necessity for, 23.
    when may issue, 24.
    form of, 25.
    variance in, 25.
EXEMPT PROPERTY,
    sale of, when void, 35.

F.

FORMALITY,
    which may be dispensed with by subsequent statute, 60.
FRAUD OF PURCHASERS,
    whether it makes their title void, or voidable merely, 40.
    not to injure innocent persons, 41.
    destroys their equitable right to subrogation, 54.
    sale void for, cannot be validated by legislature, 59.

G.

GUARDIAN,
    when may sell property without leave of court, 9.
    application in wrong county for order to sell, 10.
    foreign, sale by, 10.
    sale by, said to be *in rem*, 15.
    cannot waive service of citation on his wards, 17.
    appointment of, when void, 17.
    cannot represent conflicting interests, 17.
    consent of, to sales, 17.
    acting also as administrator, 17.
    failing to give bond, but accounting for proceeds, 22.
    sale to, or in interest of, 33.
    special statutes authorizing sales by, 65, 66-72.
    special statutes validating sales by, 56-62.

H.

HEIRS AND DEVISEES,
    nature of their interests, 56, 67.
    constitutionality of special statutes authorizing sales of their property, 63-72.

HOMESTEAD,
    sale of, when void, 35.

I.

INCOMPETENT PERSONS,
    legislature may authorize sale of their property by special statutes, 66.
    legislature may authorize conveyance of their property by special statutes, 66.

INQUISITION,
    sales without, held void, 27.

IRREGULARITIES IN SALES,
    general effect of, 21.
    made fatal by statute, 22.
    what cured by confirmation, 45.
    what cured by special curative statutes, 57, 59-60.

J.

JUDICIAL PROCEEDINGS,
    effect of, when void, 2.
    are void unless court has jurisdiction, 2, 3.
    are void if judge has no authority to act, 6.
    jurisdictional inquiries concerning, 8.
    collateral attacks upon, 8, 14, 20.
    acts interfering with, retrospectively, 57.
    acts ratifying irregular, 57.
    acts ratifying void, 58.

JUDICIAL SALES,
    defined, 1.
    irregularities in, not usually fatal, 21.
    effect of want of notice of, 28.
    by whom may be made, 29.
    at what time may be made, 30.
    at what place may be made, 31.
    failure to make at auction, 32.
    to or for person incompetent to bid, 33.
    for too great an amount, 34.
    must be confirmed by court, 43.
    right of purchasers at void, to subrogation, 51-53.
    special statutes confirming and validating, 56-62.

JUDGMENT,
    satisfied, sale under, 23, note.
    not yet rendered, sale under, 24.
    variance between, and execution, 25.

JURISDICTION,
    defined. 2.
    effect of want of, 2.
    how obtained, 3. 5.
    instances of want of, in probate courts, 4.
    not presumed in favor of, 4.
    finding of court in favor of its own jurisdiction, 4.
    over property in another state, 4.
    loss or suspension of, 7.
    loss of, by action of court of concurrent jurisdiction, 7.
    how acquired over plaintiffs, 5.
    how acquired over defendants, 5.
    how acquired in proceedings *in rem*, 5.
    how acquired in proceedings in probate, 5.
    presumptions concerning, 8.
    general rules governing inquiries concerning, 8.
    proceedings void for want of, cannot be validated, 58.

L.

LEGISLATIVE SALES,
    described, 63.
    general nature of statutes authorizing, 63.
    general remarks concerning power to authorize, 64.
    constitutionality of statutes authorizing, denied, 65.
    constitutionality of statutes authorizing, affirmed, 66.
    by guardians, 66.
    by administrators, 67.
    by trustees, foreign administrators and others, 68.
    to pay specific debts, 69.
    misapplication of proceeds of, 70.
    by person other than guardian, while there is a regularly appointed guardian, 68.
    of lands of co-tenants, 71.
    cases where they cannot be authorized, 72.

LEGISLATURE.
    restraints upon powers of, 56.
    power to validate void sales, 56-62.
    power to pass special statutes authorizing sales, 63-72.

LEVY,
    sale without, 26.

LOSS OF JURISDICTION,
    by abolishing the court, 7.
    by adjournment of the term, 7.
    by grant of administration, 7.

LOSS OF JURISDICTION—Continued.
    by final distribution of estate, 7.
    by lapse of time in which court may act, 7.

M.

MINORS,
    special statutes authorizing sales of lands of, 66.
MORTGAGE,
    reforming after foreclosure sale, 55.

N.

NOTICE OF APPLICATION TO SELL,
    absence of, not fatal in some states, 15.
    absence of, is generally fatal, 16.
    cannot be waived by a minor, 17.
    cannot be waived by a guardian, 17.
    must be given as prescribed by statute, 17, 18.
    defect in form or mode of service, 18.
    must be given for the time prescribed by law, 19.
NOTICE OF SALE,
    absence of and defects in, 28.

O.

OATH,
    failure of administrator to take, before selling, 22.
ORDERS OF SALE,
    when unnecessary, 9, 20.
    nature of proceedings to obtain, 10.
    who may petition for, 10.
    lands not embraced in, 9.
    describing lands in, 11, 20.
    effect of, as adjudication, 20.
    are void if granted without a petition, 11.
    are void if granted on insufficient petition, 11.
    cannot be collaterally attacked for error, 14, 20.
    are void if granted without proper citation, 17-19.
    contents of, 20.
    conclusive as adjudications, 20.
    to be set forth or recited in deeds, 46.

P.

PARLIAMENT,
    supreme authority of, 64.

PARTITION,
    constitutionalty of general and special laws authorizing, 71.

PERSONAL PROPERTY,
    sale of without leave of court, 9.
    deficiency of, essential to authorize sale of realty, 11.
    must be present at the sale, 31.

PETITIONS FOR ORDERS OF SALE,
    must be presented by proper person, 10.
    order without is void, 11.
    order on insufficient, is void, 11.
    what should state, 11.
    verification, omission of, 11.
    statutory provisions concerning, 12.
    liberally construed, 13.
    may refer to other papers on file, 13.
    reference to other papers, how may be made, 13.
    need not be true, 14.
    proceedings on, said to be *in rem*, 15.
    proceedings on, said to be *in personam*, 16.
    notice of, must be given, 17.
    notice of, must be given in mode prescribed, 18.
    notice of, must be given for the time prescribed, 19.

PLACE OF SALE,
    effect of sale at another place, 31.

POWERS OF SALE IN WILLS,
    who may execute, 9.

PRESUMPTIONS,
    of jurisdiction, 4, 8.
    of confirmation of sales, 43.
    that officer did his duty, 8.
    that paper not found among the files is lost, 8.

PRIVATE SALES.
    when void, 32.

PROBATE COURTS,
    instances of want of jurisdiction, 4.
    jurisdiction of, not presumed, 4.
    findings of jurisdiction, effect of, 4.
    how may acquire jurisdiction over persons, 5.
    loss of jurisdiction to proceed, 7.
    presumptions concerning jurisdiction of, 8.
    necessity of keeping up jurisdictional inquiries concerning, 9.

PROBATE PROCEEDINGS,
    are void where there is no jurisdiction over subject-matter, 4.
    have no effect beyond the state, 4.
    are void, if supposed decedent is living, 4.

PROBATE PROCEEDINGS—Continued.
  are void, if taken in the wrong county, 4.
  are void, unless jurisdiction appears, 4.
  when protected from collateral assault, 4.
  jurisdiction over persons, 5.
  presumption of jurisdiction, 8.
  must be based on sufficient petition, 11-13.
  said to be *in rem*, 15.
  said not to be *in rem*, 16.
  notice to persons in interest must be given, 16.
  must be confirmed, 43.

PROBATE SALES,
  are void if there was no valid grant of administration, 2, 7.
  are void if the estate is not subject to the probate act, 4.
  are void if the court had no jurisdiction of the subject-matter, 4.
  are void if made under order of court of another state, 4.
  are void if the supposed decedent is living, 4.
  are void if not authorized by the court, 9.
  are void if petitioned for, by person not authorized to petition, 10.
  are void if there was no petition for, 11.
  are void if the petition was insufficient, 11.
  said to be *in rem*, 15.
  void for want of notice to heirs of application for order of sale, 16-19.
  void for failure of administrator to take oath before, 22.
  void for failure of administrator to give sale bond, 22.
  void for want of appraisement, 27.
  void for want of notice of sale, 28.
  by whom may be made, 29.
  made at an improper time, 30.
  made at an improper place, 31.
  made in private, 32.
  made to person not allowed to bid, 33.
  made for too great a sum, 34.
  of property not subject to sale is void, 35.
  of property not ordered to be sold, is void, 35.
  of property in adverse possession, 38.
  made *en masse*, 39.
  effect of fraudulent practices, 40.
  effect of secret frauds, 41.
  effect of misappropriation of proceeds of sale, 41.
  effect of confirmation without notice, 42.
  necessity of confirmation, 43.
  presumption of confirmation, 43.
  right of purchaser to subrogation, 51-53.
  statutes validating invalid, 56-62.

PROCEEDS OF SALE,
    purchaser not bound to see to proper application of, 41, 70.

PURCHASERS,
    who disqualified from being, 33.
    fraudulent practices by, 40.
    not affected by secret frauds, 41.
    not bound to see to application of proceeds of sale, 41.
    at void sales, need not pay their bids, 48.
    cannot resist action for bid because of failure to title, 48.
    right to recover money paid, 49.
    right to urge estoppel arising from ratification, 50.
    right to subrogation denied, 51.
    right to subrogation sustained, 52, 53.
    right to hold lands till purchase money is refunded, 53.
    right to accounting on equitable principles, 53.
    fraud of, destroys right to subrogation, 54.

R.

RATIFICATION,
    of sales never approved in court, 43.
    of void sales, 50.
    of void sales by receiving surplus proceeds, 50.
    of void sales by acquiescence, 50.
    of void sales by minors, 50.
    of void sales by curative acts, 56-62.

REMAINDER,
    statute seeking to validate void sale of, 58.

RETROSPECTIVE LAWS,
    constitutionality of, 54.

RETURN,
    defects, variances or omissions in, 41.

RETURN OF SALES,
    confirmation cures want of verification, 44.

RETURN DAY,
    levy after, 30.
    sale after, 30.

S.

SALE,
    of property not subject to, 35.
    of different or less interest than that held by defendant, 36.
    of undesignated part, 37.
    subject to liens which do not exist, 36.

SECURITY,
: failure to give additional, effect of, 22.

SHERIFF,
: executing writ directed to another, 29.
: executing writ to which he is party, 29.

SUBROGATION,
: purchaser's right to, denied, 51.
: purchaser's right to, sustained, 52, 53.

SPECIAL STATUTES,
: confirming invalid sales and proceedings, 56-62.
: for sale of lands or minors prohibited in some States, 64.
: for compulsory sale of lands, objections to, 65.
: See CURATIVE STATUTES.
: See CONSTITUTIONALITY.
: See LEGISLATIVE SALES.

T.

TIME,
: when sale may be made, 30.
: when execution may issue, 24.

TRUSTEES,
: special acts authorizing sales by, 68.
: purchase by, at their own sales, 33.

V.

VARIANCE,
: between judgment and execution, 25.

VESTED RIGHTS,
: not to be divested by legislation, 56,
: what are, 61.

VOID JUDGMENTS,
: sale under, effect of, 2, and note.

VOID SALES,
: classified and described, 1.
: are those based on void judgments or orders, 2.
: are those made in probate without valid grant of administration, 2.
: are those made where court had no jurisdiction, 3-4.
: are those made without authority from court, 9.
: not validated by order of confirmation, 44.
: ratification of, 50.
: right of purchaser at, to resist payment of bid, 48.

VOID SALES—Continued.
    right of purchaser at, to recover money paid, 49.
    right of purchaser at, to subrogation, 51-53.
    statutes validating, 56-62.
    See **CURATIVE STATUTES**.
    See **EXECUTION SALES**.
    See **JUDICIAL SALES**.
    See **LEGISLATIVE SALES**.
    See **PROBATE SALES**.

www.ingramcontent.com/pod-product-compliance
Lightning Source LLC
Chambersburg PA
CBHW031445160426
43195CB00010BB/851